OTHERWISE

Five myths of transformation retold in verse through
the voices of women

NICOLETTA ARBIA

First published in 2020 by Restless Chipmunk

Copyright © Nicoletta Arbia 2020

ISBN 9781912892822

Also available as an ebook
ISBN 9781912892839

Typeset by Jill Sawyer Phypers
Cover design by Holly Dunn
Project management by whitefox
Printed and bound by TJ International

To Peter with deep love

CONTENTS

INTRODUCTION

I have carried this book inside me for many years without knowing. Even when it burst out of my pen I still wasn't sure what was happening. I woke up one morning with an almighty urge to write. I rushed into my study, grabbed pen and paper and went back to bed. I didn't bother to get dressed, to sit somewhere suitable or even to pull the curtains: there was no time for all that. Besides, I knew I had to remain in a cocoon of semi-darkness, of soft focus, a liminal space where things would keep flowing instead of becoming fixed.

That was the beginning of over five years of work. But the first draft of Persephone, the opening poem, was written that morning in just a couple of hours of fast, imaginative work. I believe I experienced what D.H. Lawrence meant when he said "not I but the wind that blows through me".

Persephone set the stage for the whole book. Five narrative poems exploring five Greek myths. At the centre of each poem is a woman going through a life crisis and through that crisis discovering what it takes to create change, to bring transformation and renewal.

The choice of myths has been instinctive, born out of my childhood impressions. I remember a primary school book with a picture of Kore being dragged into the Underworld. She looked beautiful, she burnt with life yet she had to go down a black hole… And what about Psyche? I was fascinated by the prohibition against looking into the face of the God. Why? How can you trust without checking?

Mythological stories often seemed to me stranger and more compelling than fairy tales. Retelling them in poetry seems to capture more powerfully their essence. Poetry is the language of the ineffable and it's through such media that myths reveal themselves to me.

The title of the book tells us that things are never what we expect them to be. It is always otherwise. Persephone's existence has been turned upside down. She's lost everything, her life seems over but it is otherwise. Her experience transforms her from a naïve, carefree girl into a mature woman; from someone who expects liberation from the outside to someone able to look into her depths, discover personal power and find her place in a Universe where all things are interconnected.

It is the same for Psyche. She believes that her trials are meant to destroy her but it is otherwise. The trials are the making of her. Through them she learns to renegotiate the balance of power between her inner feminine and her inner masculine. This operation, known in alchemy as Coniunctio, makes human beings whole and it's part of the larger aim of alchemy, which is the reconciliation of opposites: masculine and feminine, outer and inner, past and present, spirit and matter, conscious and unconscious, reason and imagination, ego and soul.

It is only through the reconciliation of opposites that we can become "unstuck" and resolve the burgeoning, pressing problems of a modern world in which everything has become more and more polarised.

For Psyche the reconciliation of opposites also passes through reconciling pain and joy. She becomes more able to embrace both in the now and it's when we do that that we live life fully, that we experience less avoidance and anxiety, more presence and gratitude.

Balancing the masculine and feminine principles is a theme running through most of the five myths. If for Psyche it is a matter of developing the masculine capacities for shaping things, accepting power (but not more than needed) and being single-minded, for Persephone and Ariadne it is about not to expect damnation or salvation from the outside but to take responsibility and stand on one's own feet. Taking responsibility always entails the withdrawal of projections without which it is usually impossible to see the truth of any given situation.

Cassandra, instead, needs to tap into the feminine quality of compassion and empathy and, similarly, for Theseus it is about finding his masculine strength without losing the capacity to connect. The thread that guides him out of the labyrinth starts shining when he cries, when he recognises the Minotaur as part of himself, as his shadow side. Unfortunately the feminine qualities of compassion and insight are not anchored in him and after the trial of the labyrinth only a stronger masculine is left in the driving seat. Devoid of emotional courage, Theseus is unable to be truthful. He can't tell Ariadne that during the urgency of those turbulent times he believed he loved her but it was just a short-lived illusion. Illusions must be recognised and faced if one wants to sustain a stable, loving relationship.

Eurydice portrays the complex dance of relationship. Orpheus plays out his masculine principle by concentrating on music and the outer world; Eurydice plays out her feminine principle by concentrating on the inner dimension and the relationship which is too much at the centre of her life. He feels burdened; she feels neglected. In the end, despite some moving towards the middle on her part, the polarisation almost breaks them up and it takes a crisis as big as death to shake both out of the established patterns. Only then, after Eurydice's death, is Orpheus aware of what he has lost and ready to begin a long soul-searching journey.

It seems that all journeys towards maturity (what Carl Jung calls Individuation) are triggered and fuelled by suffering. The descent into the Underworld is a thread that runs through most of the five myths. Indeed, suffering pushes us to leave the surface of things and take the risk of diving into those deep, dark places (the labyrinth is another symbol for them) where the seeds of renewal are hidden. Here we can shed the narrow concerns of the ego and find what it is that is meaningful to us. Here we have the opportunity to turn poison into medicine.

Cassandra doesn't descend into the Underworld but her tragic life itself feels like walking in the Underworld. From the beginning she is focussed on the transcendent, on a mystical vocation that is at odds with the expectations of the world. After a life spent trying to keep a tight grip on things the only way forward is to surrender to the Unknown. Her God has been hidden and as she approaches death, Cassandra manages to let go. She used to be so opinionated but now she can't go for yes and she can't go for no. She stops trying to understand. It's not the mind that must be her guide but the heart and the pull of mystery.

Recently I have reflected on the biblical story of Jacob wrestling with the angel. Jacob is a very imperfect human being as he cheats his brother Esau out of his inheritance. We might define him a liar and a "grabber". The crucial event in the story takes place many years after the misdeed. Jacob is on the bank of the river Jabbok. He is being chased by his father-in-law, with whom he has unresolved issues, and on the other side of the water Esau, who has vowed to kill him, is waiting for revenge. Jacob can't move forward and can't move backwards. He is trapped with hardly any choice left. He sends his family and all his possessions across the water and remains on the spot, stripped of everything, alone, as night begins to fall… then this mysterious being comes and Jacob wrestles with him until daybreak to be left victorious but wounded. The wound, to his hip, will make him limp for the rest of his life.

The angel is a gift but Jacob doesn't immediately know that. We know little while we walk the way of the wound. As we go through a Dark Night of the Soul we can rarely see the light at the end of the tunnel and we usually don't understand what it is all about. Yet, all that is needed is to welcome our experience as Jacob did – our fear, vulnerability, loneliness and awareness of our shortcomings. It is when we are weak that we are strong.

It is when we accept the limitation and face the pain, when we hold the opposites inside ourselves that we meet the Divine in our life. Just like the alchemist we turn the base metal, the raw material, into gold. There's no gold without the raw material.

Perfection and imperfection are as inextricably intertwined as the pain and joy Psyche would like to pull apart. In the crucible of life you can't have the one without the other. That's why at the end of the myth Psyche is worthy of the God. What counts is that by now she is engaged in a process of self-development, it doesn't matter if she seems to be making the same mistake again, if she is still looking at something she was told not to look at. It doesn't matter if she's still got the hubris of wanting payback. We can afford to fall and get up a million times as long as we are honest about our mistakes and keep working on ourselves.

I think that the struggle Jacob is engaged in is between the ego and the Soul (which is our deep core, the God within) and the wound he receives is to the ego. Carl Jung warns that the experience of the Soul is always a defeat for the ego. So Jacob's ego gets smaller, Jacob empties out and so paradoxically he can be permanently wounded yet victorious, like the seed that must die in order to bear fruit.

The wound speaks to me of compassion. The heart has broken open and when that happens there's no way back so the wound is permanent and it changes Jacob's identity: he will receive a new name and God's blessing.

I had a dream last year. In the dream I am at secondary school. Each student sits on her or his own beautiful carpet (an image for the Soul). At the end of lessons the carpets are rolled up and stored away but something happens and I lose mine. When, not without effort, I manage to enter the room where the carpets are kept, I see that it is huge and packed to the ceiling. It's like looking for a needle in a haystack. But the worst thing is that I no longer remember what my carpet looks like. I fear I will never be able to find it again. I feel devastated.

After much thrashing about I find a teacher willing to help.

She gets a little three-pronged key. I follow her anxiously. She is small, nondescript and limps conspicuously. I find myself thinking: "She is disabled, she knows suffering, and because of that she will take me to the right place."

Ariadne's story ends with a dream. She dreams of Dionysus and then, when she wakes up, she finds Him right in front of her. Ariadne has had the courage to defy the sick family and society she comes from and has lost everything as a result. Now, in her emptiness, she's made space for the new, she's ready for ecstasy, for the life of Dionysus. He will help her harness her wild, free nature, the nature of someone whose wounds, to quote Hephaestus, belong to the Inner Fire.

PERSEPHONE

Even in the time of waning, in the weeks of our gradual change
nothing could ever again help us to fulfilment, except
our own solitary course over the sleepless landscape.

R. M. RILKE

Synopsis

The nymph Kore is taking a walk in the valley. While she is busy picking flowers suddenly the ground opens beneath her feet and Hades, the Lord of the Dead, grabs her and drags her down into His dark kingdom.

From this point on she will have to negotiate a very different life from the one she was used to. Her mother, Demeter, Goddess of harvest and fertility, plots to free her, and when all Her efforts are frustrated She responds by bringing eternal winter over the land.

In time Kore comes to embrace her Destiny, she becomes Persephone, loving bride of Hades and Queen of the Underworld. She will spend six months of the year in the Underworld and six months on the Earth. When she is down it is autumn and winter, when, to Demeter's joy, she resurfaces, she brings spring and summer.

Traditionally this is the myth that dramatises the origin of seasons.

Characters

Kore/Persephone
A nymph, the daughter of Demeter. In the Underworld her name changes to Persephone.

Hades
King of the Dead. He reigns in the Underworld. He is Kore's kidnapper.

Demeter
Goddess of Fertility and Harvest, mother of Kore.

Apollo
God of Light and Darkness, Healing, Music, Poetry and Prophecy.

I
Kore

Why has this happened to me?
Why?
I trouble myself looking for an explanation.
Maybe because I had mistaken for purity
the naivety in which my heart was dwelling?
Or because my orange garments lifted every day
like froth in the cool porthole of illicit thoughts?
Or maybe it was because when I was dancing
I felt driven by the uncontrolled will
of my youth?
Or was it because I was too sensitive in treading the Earth,
too exposed to the delusions of Time,
too defenceless before the impermanence of all things,
too loving
or flirtatious?

I felt as fragile as a twig.
I suffocated,
I twisted in the snake-like,
powerful grip of the God.

I was like a flower brutally cut,
a shoot uprooted
by the sidereal Flood.
Quashed if I struggled,
lashed if I dared resist,
I was taken over by a force
as fast and decisive as lightning,
and I disappeared into
a terrifying pit
of blindness and silence,

and I passed out,
and I went limp in the violent arms of the God
like (the horror) a newly born baby
in the arms of its mother.

II
Persephone

Coming round I am in His
presence.
With what power of feeling
or regret
can one look upon
such a remote being?

Will He kill me if I show fear?
But my body already betrays me
and shakes uncontrollably.
Will He kill me if I contradict Him?
If I declare to detest Him and His
world of ineffable shadows?

Before this lunar monster,
this master of owls,
this alien power
enclosed in the Earth's muscles
I feel fear
I feel terror.
I don't want to end my days in a grave!
Someone please help me!

My mother won't allow it.
She is as much a deity as You are
I scream at Him with my eyes.
My mother will save this life of mine
and all its vibrant hopes,
She will get my shapeless adolescence
out of this abyss!

But time passes and I'm still here.
How many months? Maybe three, maybe four
it's difficult to say without the Sun...
and yet they say that the Sun lies here
and from here he goes out every morning
on his exulting coach of light.
How is it possible for the Sun to love Darkness so much?
If Light and Darkness are so intertwined
what would that mean?
Contamination and Oblivion?
Or a hidden, common essence of all things?

My mind's labours to understand
look like a tangle of brier in which I stumble.

And yet
more and more often
I let my brow rest,
lie in the blue-grey light
that pervades all like pure sea water;
and the walls...
oh, for weeks on end I did not notice
their strange, amber beauty
as if they were pregnant
with ancient,
sublime memories.
I have no familiarity
with the feelings which visit me,
untimely,
anxiety-generating:
not nostalgia for the Earth
but pride and compassion
in attending the evolving inner rhythms
of the Shadows,
in catching the wavelength

of their thoughts,
it's as if I had known them all for ever
and had for ever been
mother.
Mother?
Or beloved bride.
Whose bride?
Of the monster who holds sway here?

I am ashamed of being fascinated by Him.
He visits me
tender and absolute,
distant and omnipresent
and every time I look at Him
something happens inside me,
something I can't decipher…
like a deepening of the heart,
a going far into myself.
The journey is *mine*,
I am the pilgrim going through *my own* Universe,
I reserve nothing for Him
yet it is He who triggers my steps.
I can't forbid
nor disown
this bitter spark
that comes from Him,
that makes me grow,
that confers to my light brow
a heavy reflection of Eternity.
There,
touching Eternity,
it changes you for ever…
hearing the peacock's scream,
guessing the whereabouts of the phoenix' nest,
shelling the pomegranates

at first with hatred
then with possessive astonishment…

When He comes
I don't know how to behave:
should I be acting the violated prisoner,
the wounded child,
should I hit Him with sinister rage,
show incurable pain?
But I don't know what to do.
By now my feelings of aversion
are left as small pockets
of rejection
in an ever increasing desire for Him
with which I cannot reason.

Oh, I wish I could be like the Sun
and integrate the two worlds!
If only someone negotiated this for me:
on my own I can't,
I can't negotiate anything...
and yet
and yet
perhaps He would listen to me,
perhaps He would let me go:
six months on the Earth among flowers and palms
and six months here exploring who I am,
placating this longing for
knowledge
that on the fifth month presses and grows inside me
as if I were pregnant.

I am pregnant through Him.
Persephone He calls me,
not Kore.

He has changed my name
like in an initiation.
I am pregnant with something
that resembles Mercy
and makes me move
with an absorbed heart,
with such Grace as I've never known before.
I feel like a Queen,
Queen of those who have lived
and of those who will,
Queen of this mysterious coming and going
of souls
because, I have found out,
He doesn't hold on to anyone
not even me.

My mother up there weeps and plots
to free me.
I hear Her
the way one hears the potent, filtered voice
of one's dreams.
Oh Demeter,
oh my darling,
oh caring mother,
I am a prisoner of nothing
but what it's left for me to understand.

And now every time He visits me
I pronounce His name.

His name has the powerful taste
of the Earth's bowels,
of submerged volcanos,
of psychosis
and sanity,

of continuous alarm
like before Death,
because He is Death.
This I knew from the start.

But now I know the Regeneration
that He establishes and protects
like a tender monarch who issues laws
to assist the weak
and weak we all are.

Regeneration is His unbreakable rule,
it fills the sharp rock of this world
like water fills the curved bed of the sea.

The happiness that washed over me on Earth
(like a marvel due to me)
used to leave me inert,
cut off as under a glass bell
and I used to breathe duality.

It's no longer all I wish
because the unity of all things
has blown its wind in my hair
and has composed me in the iconic posture
in which all the generations to come
will imagine me:
with loose, intricate locks,
enamelled, cave-like cloak,
the pomegranate broken open in my hand
and that reluctant attitude
between giving and receiving,
between resistance and abandon
which is the last duality left to me…
because,

despite everything,
I still can't let go.

I asked Him
how do you let go,
how do you fully embrace your own path.
In my despair,
in my eagerness to cover the last stretch of the road
(but will it be the last?),
I asked Him to take me,
to penetrate me,
to give me sexual ecstasy,
fusion.
I asked Him to literally make me pregnant
without sparing me
but consuming and burning me
in the crucible of the cosmic
passion
I read in His eyes.
I already feel that fiery sword
piercing my body
and the infinite relief of being at last
in His loving,
protective arms.

But He does not move.
He is unemotional.
Is He rejecting me?
I'm furious!

You kidnapped me,
You wanted me here,
it wasn't me who orchestrated everything,
horrendous monster,
traitor,

it's *You* Duality,
it's Y*ou* the two-faced one,
shameless hypocrite
what did you think You could teach me?
You have nothing to teach me
except the contradictions
of a pagan tyrant!

Oh! It feels like I'm crying even more tears than before.
Between the fifth and the sixth month
I feel more lost than ever.
Not even right after the abduction
was I so desperate
because now I have nothing left,
not even my dignity,
not even my clarity of purpose.

All,
all is an incomprehensible vortex,
all is lost.

Catharsis,
give me a moment of catharsis
like a balm for my wound,
give me respite
icy Gorgons,
Furies of unrest as drunk as Dionysus,
I am no longer myself!

Or maybe I am myself for the first time?
Who can say?
I wept all my tears
and when I calmed down
He came once more.
He had a cloak of stars.

I was surprised
yet stars are His prerogative,
I knew this at the start
why am I surprised?
I try not to be surprised by anything anymore.
Trembling I sit in His presence.
Does He want me standing?
Like a King who demands respect?
An Emperor who mercilessly scrutinises me?
As if I had failed...
I am full of failings,
of unreasonable omissions,
of broken vows
and impetuous flaws,
there's even the odd crime,
surely I don't deserve His attention,
what a strange idea I had nurtured!

But why
why this feeling
that He doesn't do anything,
that I am the one doing all of it,
that everything,
everything unfolds inside me
in the immense arena
of *my* brutal will,
of *my* capacity or incapacity for love,
of *my* unripe mind:
a rosary of thoughts and ruminations
that paralyses me
and cuts me off from life.

My crying is now subdued.
No more dramas.
I strip myself of everything,

I abandon any hope
of fruition,
but I am not sad,
it is freeing.
I sit quiet and solemn
in the modesty of the present moment
which is all that matters.

I watch the Shadows flow.
In this world they are a discreet
but uninterrupted sight.
They stroke your skin day and night,
if you can call it day.
Immersed in their constant passing
you can become
accustomed to their touch,
or stay sensitive
to the unfolding of their destinies.
I want to remain sensitive to the destinies of the Universe
whose strings they pull.
Oh no, I can't abdicate!
Abdicate? I really do speak like a Queen.

To them I will open up the obscure centre
of my Experience:
Warning and Prophecy,
Adventure
and Delivery.
These are the labour pains,
like an earthquake in the belly.
I am delivering myself.
And when everything is fulfilled
and the end of the sixth month will strike,
I will resurface on the Earth
as if released by a glorious dream.

I will not need to ask anyone's permission,
not even His,
He, who now looks moved,
and certainly not my mother's,
She who has worked so hard to save me
without knowing that it wasn't necessary.
Concluded the gestation,
fulfilled the mystic date,
maybe I will be like the Sun
who
with perpetual motion,
watchful and aware,
in the Unity of the Worlds and of all opposites,
from Darkness rises
and in Darkness lies.

EURYDICE

In order to arrive at what you do not know
You must go by a way which is the way of ignorance.
In order to possess what you do not possess
You must go by the way of dispossession.

T. S. ELIOT

Synopsis

Orpheus, son of the muse Calliope, was an amazing musician. He could play the lyre like no other and had a melodious voice that enchanted both humans and beasts. Not even inanimate objects could resist the ecstasy of his music, the whole of creation yearned for it.

When Orpheus met Eurydice, a beautiful arboreal nymph, he fell in love with her and the two got married. However, sometime after the wedding, while she was walking in the countryside, Eurydice was bitten by a snake and died from the poison.

After that Orpheus was never the same. He grieved for a long time and nothing could bring him comfort. Eventually he decided he would go into the Underworld and get his bride back. He went armed only with his lyre and his voice, and when he arrived he played so powerfully and movingly that even Hades was touched. Hades promised Orpheus that Eurydice could follow him back into the world of the living, but warned him that he must walk ahead and must not turn to look at her until they were both out into the light. If he looked too soon he would lose his wife for ever.

Sadly Orpheus did just that and Eurydice was irretrievably plunged back into the Kingdom of the Dead.

From then on Orpheus roamed the Earth in ever deepening despair while shunning all women.

Eventually a group of Maenads killed him and tore him apart. He was buried in a river and Zeus turned his lyre into a constellation.

Characters

Eurydice
Orpheus' wife. She is an arboreal nymph.

Orpheus
Eurydice's husband and son of the muse Calliope. He is an accomplished musician.

Asclepius
Son of Apollo. God of Medicine and Healing.

Apollo
God of Light and Darkness, Healing, Music, Poetry and Prophecy.

Hades
King of the Underworld.

Persephone
Queen of the Underworld.

Charon
He carries the souls of the newly dead across the river Styx into the Underworld.

Maenads
Female followers of the God Dionysus. They roam the countryside performing frenzied, ecstatic dances. When possessed by the God they have tremendous strength which allows them to tear apart both animals and humans.

I
The way we were

Whenever I looked at you, Orpheus,
a new flush of youth
seemed to light up your face
flooding it with a quality
which, I knew,
would withstand the future,
the wear and tear
of life
and time.

Whenever I looked at you, Orpheus,
your body,
froth of light and muscles,
seemed first to expand
then to grow thin
surging towards the treetops
in one singular votive gesture.

That you had wandered for centuries
on my sensual paths
devoid of devotion or discernment,
without ever meeting me,
never caused me grief.
I never felt you had disdained me,
treated me with irreverence.
Those had been times too virgin
for normal human understanding.
I wouldn't have been ready to know you,
I wouldn't have raised myself
out of my arboreal mysteries,
out of my drawn out slumber.

The ineluctability of awakening,
of the love match,
the call of Fate,
all came later.
Your voice was echo and mediator,
your music a slow, liberating ecstasy
replacing that childhood
I had never lived.

I was already an adult
when I appeared
or so I felt
whenever, from the melancholic hive
of my heart,
as from a window,
I observed History,
and saw its wild features,
its crude, material flow.

Oh! I didn't know what to do.
I was spellbound,
paralysed by the incomprehensible gap
between the audacity of action
that History demanded
and my inner light,
the pure, shapeless gestures
I was used to,
the absorbed slowness of my limbs
on which only the wind
could sometimes impress
an urgency of movement.
The wind which shakes willows and roses,
oaks and poplars
guiding them from season to season

in solemn,
pre-ordained procession.

It was you, Orpheus, who filled the gap
by recognising who I was,
by dragging me into the ecstasy
of your pilgrimage
and by showing me your tribute
of surrender to the inexplicable.

Through your love
I tried out History,
I accepted myself,
I sidestepped my inhibitions,
laughed at the mayhem of life,
fed on its ephemeral blessings,
lay with equanimity
under the weight of ambitions and losses,
learnt how to make solemn
the excruciating incoherence of days.

Sometimes my voice
reaching for notes it had not yet found,
would achieve a resonance
that married the accents
of your lyre
with deep intensity.

In those moments your mother Calliope came to mind,
perfect muse,
prime inspiration,
inexhaustible fountain of Peace.

Oh Orpheus!
I became mirror of your soul

and unexpected heart of your hopes.
I became dream of premonition,
apex of your wandering
whose mystic fruit
would coagulate,
would become real
only through the extreme test.

As I slowly came to understand,
the love you demanded and gave
would never become
exclusive tenderness,
sealed, historic exchange:
it was more like a daily seduction
overturned by hurricanes.
They swept you out
of the dazzling circle
of our embraces
into the Absolute of Being.
Like Dawn,
you used to leave our sanctum
and spread everywhere
always impervious to being part of a couple,
always oblivious of the meeting point
I constantly pursued.
You would do this
either with an intolerant yearning for freedom
or with neutral argument.
And so the slow,
pressing,
alchemical evolution of our relationship
brought *me* down to earth
you up towards celestial worlds.
I learnt the secrets
of passion

and human existence,
you felt increasingly complete
in the abstraction of the Firmament,
in the remote swirling
of Music and Intellect,
sources at which Creation would drink
as at the tolls of the healing bells
of young Asclepius,
of merciful Apollo.

II
Death

In time
I was reduced to wandering all day long
in the countryside,
bathed in its soft
enduring greenery,
dazed by its scents,
overwhelmed
by its lush,
symbiotic power.
I wanted to be drunk with it all,
to have nothing to think about,
I wanted to throw a bridge
between my arboreal and my human life,
I wanted to forget you, Orpheus!

I moved barefooted
looking for places contrary to Reason:
not superficial clearings
but thick tangles
like untamed animals,
briers
and enamelled grass.
I touched tree trunks
with twisted bark
and deep roots
on which I rested
fingers hungry for moss,
lips thirsty for resin.

They say
it was a small, green snake

that bit me
but, in my imagination,
I saw a powerful creature rear up in front of me
like a hissing cobra.

To this day
reptile is a word that breaks my spine
and sends me into oblivion.

The snake attacked with the determination
of an irate Zeus,
it left me devoid of the doubts
which had always plagued my life.

I ran like crazy
in an electric panic
of the mind,
in an asthmatic thud
of the lungs.
My blood turned to poison,
My body became death's unwilling lover
and all,
all of this passed through me
like the unredeemed remnant
of a life draining away,
a life becoming other people's memory
before having known itself.

I screamed in a voice louder than thunder,
I issued a call mad with need,
I no longer wished to forget you, Orpheus,
I wanted to remember everything!
Oh! I refused to become lost,
to get wrenched
from inside out,

dismembered in the discoloured,
blunt vortex
of the approaching Nothing.

You heard me like the Mind finally hears the Soul,
like the adult hears the child
reciting its own abandonment.
You immediately knew where I was
and came back to me
on the glistening thread that linked us,
in the symbiosis
of the contradictory inner space
piercing
and hypnotising us.

You found me
supine on the plain
in the already diverging
immensity of Time
and in the agony of the moment,
in the frantic pain firing our eyes with tears,
I understood how the tapestry of History
takes shapes,
dissolves
and gets recreated.
Through my own personal dissolution
I touched the eternal jigsaw
to which we, unaware but assiduous,
devote everything.

To the end, like in a dream,
I felt the tender, ferocious grip
of your arms
locked around the body I was leaving,
passage of terror and surrender.

The lyre
was the last thing I heard
but whether real or already a memory
I couldn't say.
I floated away on its familiar, ripe sound.

The veils opened and closed behind me
like winged doors
with invisible locks.

Oh yes, once I touched the bottom of the sea,
the ultimate point of incarnation,
I could only go up again towards the Source.

In the blind pitch of the eyes
I was engulfed by ecstasy.

III
The Underworld

First Movement

Oh Orpheus,
you wandered for years looking for me,
blind,
deaf to the remoulding of life,
greedy for memories,
prostrated by the humble truth of your pain,
wrapped in the long sob of Time
which never seemed to heal you.

I could see you
through the wavy crystal
of the knowledge I was granted.
Your languishing pelted my walls
deranging with guilty
compassion
the altar of my experience.

I was consoled only when your lyre,
fired by my absence,
displayed with sharp cries the universal loss
and in it all the hostility of the world
was appeased,
all the furies and false ideals of the people
seemed to linger,
to stall
like demons made inert, unreal
by the love prism.

Eventually,
pruned, strengthened by suffering,

you were ready to look for me where I really was.
But where was I?
Did I know?
What did I know more than you?
I who sometimes lay
in a similar miasma of regret
and opacity,
I who feared seeing you again
as one fears unleashing a judgement:
that you would recoil
disappointed by the incorporeal.

Oblique, demanding,
intense, demure,
"I haven't changed!
Don't come!
I am not worth it!"

And yet I have changed:
disentangled from earthly reverberations,
here I am spacious with light
and as tall as a birch.

Touched by the Divine
I have gathered myself
on the uncomfortable threshold
of a new way to love.
Here, at times,
I experience the breath of Spirit:
profound
contemplative and devastating.
Here I fluctuate on the abyss
which regenerates us all
and for which there are no words.

Oh Orpheus,
shamanic and irresistible groom,
crystal child,
heart of dove,
even Hermes stands mindful of you
and foresees your coming
as flood of river and celestial commotion.
Hermes whose gaze falls on me
with absorbed, quiet complicity.

"You winged guide who walks between the worlds
help Orpheus," I pray,
"help him
because if he comes he must understand
that dying before dying is the most necessary thing
but also the most difficult.
Help him
because he thinks he is looking for me
when in truth he is looking for himself."
He comes to claim me
as the Mind finally claims the Soul.
He comes to claim me
because I am his guide
now brimming with both discernment
and devotion.

Second Movement

Oh what a vision!
I saw Orpheus
descending into the Underworld
like a ray of sun,
a fisher of souls with a heart full of thorns!
How changed he was!
Distraught and gaunt,

vulnerable,
transparent like ether,
like stars,
and yet more earthy,
more recognisable,
more attuned to his destiny,
more intertwined with life.

He couldn't see me
but I could see him from afar,
already he was playing the lyre
which is his shelter and his gift.
The music poured in,
it kept increasing, amplifying,
a forerunner of arcane beauty.
The invisible World
drank it
from North to South
from East to West
without distinction
between Tartarus and Elysian Fields.
It reunified the Universe,
it seduced each soul:
a human grace
as powerful as the divine.
"How is that possible?
How is that possible?" I cried,
"and if so, what is not possible?"
Even Hades' ebony throne
was shaking like a living thing
and I felt my heart
soar in joyous bursts
like a newly liberated hawk.

At last there was silence
and Orpheus lay at Persephone's feet.
She was the only other woman he had ever loved
and by looking at him I could not tell
whether he had come to beg
or only to bow in stillness
on the threshold of
Eternity.

Persephone looked suffused
with solar light:
they were the kisses She received from Demeter
every six months,
on parting,
and She was almost crying
tender as the violets in Her hair,
blessed with a majesty that was not solemn
but intimate and burning.
She and Hades were sitting hand in hand.
"I beg you,"
I heard Her whisper to Him,
"let's give him the choice."

"The choice?" I thought,
"what choice?
He is here for me",
and a strange wave of panic washed over me
but there was no time to wander
because there and then
the veils dropped
and a feverish, bewildering closeness
engulfed us,
me diaphanous,
Orpheus solid,
me sparkling with celestial light,

him worn out by the thousand steps taken.
The fear of not being saved turned into confusion:
how could I follow him
when I hadn't even drunk of Lethe?
I was still awash with the memories
of my wandering on the paths of the Earth
and of the inexplicable vitality of Death.

Oh! I started to follow him
but at every step I made
the conflict pressed on me.
I wanted to go back to life
but perhaps I was not ready to cope again with Earth
and I had an intuition that no cycle can be rushed,
shortened,
moulded to our needs.

And we were walking one behind the other
towards life on Earth
like lovers
and enemies
panting with impatience,
exulted by the heroic enterprise we were unwrapping,
coy and reluctant,
tripping,
trembling,
constantly on the cusp of a scream,
of a call to one another,
of a prayer.
But our voices weren't coming out
and he could not look at me:
Hades had decreed that if he were to turn
he would lose me!

This then is the choice:

he can still turn and pull our destinies apart,
leave me here for ever…?!

I felt the orb of his uncertainty
mirror mine
and flow backwards
towards me
like a broken vow.
I felt the doubt
clawing at him
that I might not be following,
only emptiness and enigma
behind him.
Oh what is it that we call Faith,
what is it?

A livid wind got up
blowing from the Styx
river of stricken night,
frontier of amaranth and dark seaweeds
in the heart of the Dead,
in the all-knowing woods of the ancestors,
in the wild germination
of caresses
held back for years.

"Don't run! Wait!
What will you say to Charon?
What will we tell him?
That he can ferry us backwards
in the unwelcoming clog
of his sneer,
that we can get out,
resurface
like an anointed breeze,

like balm for the bells?
It's all madness!
Don't run!
I don't want to get to the crucial moment
when we may find out
that there's no choice,
that we deluded ourselves,
that Hades is making a joke of us
and Persephone is jealous of me!
Oh here we are, I too lack Faith!
Please don't run
because I don't know what to do:
our adventure is burning too fast
like a blink of the eyes,
like a beat the heart has skipped,
I can't do it like this!
I need time!

Oh Time!
It's never enough:
it comes to us from all corners
but it is always a bitter voice,
a red hot ghost
slipping through our fingers
in a duel of intentions
and naked labyrinths.

With nightmarish sigh
the wind from the Styx
increases and freezes me.
I am a balking animal,
a unicorn who doesn't want to go back
to being a mere horse.
And yet I want to be reunited with you, Orpheus,
I want *you*

only *you*
because for the first time
I have seen
the mystical splendour of your Soul,
the honey of your eyes,
the contemplative strength of your hands
and the tension of your steep flanks…

Oh! Suddenly,
in the listening,
in the proffered, loving listening
of all my fibres
I hear,
I know
that you will turn
because dying before dying
is not coming down into the Underworld
to save me
but is being able,
while alive,
to sustain Death's gaze,
Death
who teaches all,
quickens all,
changes all,
turns everything inside out.'

IV
Solutio

The moment has gone
and it is the dream that remains,
a slow eavesdropping
at the doors of the Future.

But the Future is so long
and scattered,
locked in fragments.

You turned
and I disappeared
like a burst bubble,
like dying twice.

Goodbye
and the veils sprang up again
in a mutiny of all senses.

Now,
through the Oracle that's opening up,
I get the mournful image
of a man dismembered
and sacrificed
to his inner feminine destiny.

Only the lyre,
vertical and open constellation,
reminds me
that nothing has been lost,
that all is a path
to knowledge
spiralling,

devoid of shortcuts,
living and dying revealing themselves
one and the same thing:
a time made of terse experiencing
and infinite imprints of love.

ARIADNE

My shy moonshadow would willingly
speak to my sunshadow from afar
in the language of fools
in between I, lit up sphynx,
creating stillness to the right and to the left
both shadows I have generated.

R. M. RILKE

Synopsis

Queen Pasiphae of Crete slept with a bull sent by Zeus and gave birth to the Minotaur, a creature half man half bull. Minos, the king, angry and ashamed but reluctant to kill the monster, hid it in a labyrinth constructed by Daedalus. The labyrinth was so intricate that no one, once inside, could ever find the way out.

Androgeus, son of Minos, went to Athens to participate in the Panathenaic Games but was killed in an accident. Minos, furious at the loss of his son, demanded the sacrifice of seven men and seven women: this was the number of Athenian youths who were supposed to be sent every year as food for the Minotaur.

The story begins three years later when Theseus, son of the king of Athens, decides to be one of the seven men. He intends to go and slay the monster. He doesn't realise that even if he did manage to kill the Minotaur he would never be able to exit the labyrinth.

Princess Ariadne, daughter of Minos, falls in love with Theseus and decides to help him. She obtains a magical ball of yarn forged by the God Hephaestus and gives it to Theseus to unravel during his journey into the labyrinth.

Theseus kills the Minotaur and by following the thread manages to retrace his steps back and out of the labyrinth.

Theseus sails back home taking Ariadne with him but during a stop at the island of Naxos he decides to abandon Ariadne whom he leaves asleep on the beach.

When Ariadne wakes up she has to face the pain of Theseus's betrayal but the God Dionysus comes to her and makes her His happy, immortal bride.

Characters

Ariadne
Daughter of King Minos and Queen Pasiphae of Crete.

Theseus
Son of the King of Athens.

The Minotaur
A monster half man and half bull generated by Queen Pasiphae.

Hephaestus
God of Fire. He is a blacksmith who makes weapons and military equipment for the other Gods. He was born lame.

Chiron
One of the Centaurs. Son of a Titan and a sea nymph, he is famous for his wisdom and knowledge of medicine. Chiron tutored the young Theseus in the healing and military arts.

Dionysus
God of Wine, Vegetation, Pleasure, Festivity, Ecstasy and Madness.

I
The Lament of Ariadne

Standing on this ridge
I watch the sea
crumpled and stern
faithful mirror of my own defeated soul.

I walk to this place every day.
With broken gaze
I scan the waves arching in the sunlight,
I look at a land that is my mother:
clay of my clay
flower of my flower
but that now I must disown.
In front of the sea I feel the convulsion
of my solitude,
the weight of the curse.
I stagger in front of so much
evil.
I can't believe what is happening,
it turns the island into a nest of murderers
and my father into something worse than a demon.
Oh world! You used to be healthy
now you are sick and rotten,
an undomesticated charnel house,
a necropolis of barbarous spits.

Where and how was the egg of the snake hatched?
With the stinking protection of which God
has this plot gone
from ephemeral, bad dream
to corrupt, unassailable reality?
My blood drums in my temples

like the galloping of a horse gone mad,
my feet sink in this blood-soaked soil
like in the quicksand of a destiny
before which I have no key
or voice.

And I'm the only one who appears to care.
The whole of Crete looks oblivious
to the presence of a man-eating monster.
They seem to have forgotten
that the Queen herself, my mother, has generated it,
that it's the King, my father, who wants the tribute of lives…
all of them come and go
like nothing is happening:
exemplary and myopic subjects
happily ensconced
in the immoral void
of an integrity shattered by ignorance
and fear,
by the rousing of ancestral flattery
and unconscious,
vicarious,
collective revenge.

Oh, this is wasted land
made of decayed teeth
and grim admonitions!
If spring stopped coming
I wouldn't be surprised,
if summer turned into cracking drought,
I would recognise the neat, unerring hand of justice
whose chalice
sooner or later
we are meant to empty.

Yet, unexpectedly,
tears don't come when I launch myself
into the dark, uprooted kernel
of pain and prophecy
but when,
near the sea,
crouched on the steepest rock,
I feel the golden breath of childhood,
the modulated, sweet currents
of lost innocence,
then my aching rage,
the strident voice of the inner judge,
becomes again the pliable essence
of a child
and, either lost in my mother's lap,
or propped up by the bold gaiety
conferred by fatherly love,
I try
I try to pray.
I can no longer identify the cycles of my life,
tell past from present,
but I sacrifice myself
to the vertiginous knowledge
that there is,
there must be a way
of redeeming this life,
of leaving dusk
and darkness behind
to dwell once again
in tenderness.

II
The Black Sails

Only at night do I look around
because by day I cannot bear
the anguish
dripping from the sails.

The black sails
are an aching,
rugged cobweb
crowded with death.

Only at night do I look around
because by day I cannot bear
the expectation
of so many lives due to be cut down in their prime.
They are looking to me,
to me,
Theseus,
because I am the one who will fight to save them.

This battle inflames me,
generates my tomorrow,
never mind if I am alone
to hold the hope,
to snatch the arcane spark
that destiny proffers,
a destiny that crushes my shoulders with the roses of yesterday.

Oh father,
you didn't want me to leave
but I am not a boy any more.
As a man I watch the sea,
as a man I scan the waves

arching in the moonlight,
dwelling in the mirror
of my sleepless eyes.

I am not a boy any more
and this thirst for liberation
and victory
pours from heart to body
like libation
blessed by the Gods.

For two days they've been saying we are approaching Crete:
it's something in the colour of the water,
in the flight of the birds,
in the thread of dreams.

Oh, I am not a boy any more
and I have proved this
not once but several times!
Let me, father,
let me keep watch
in the impervious cradle of the night,
motionless at the still closed doors
of all my Ideals.
Let me open the flower of prophecy
petal by petal
in the hive of intractable terrors and darings,
in the red hot scream
that shakes my veins and wrists
Land!
Land!

III
The Landing

I saw them disembark
and touch land.
They already carried
a spasm of ash,
a ruinous essence,
the halo of their death sentence.

I am standing close to my father
in the royal seat,
the breeze is swelling my dress
drenching it in the blue of the sky.

Tears prick my eyes
like pins or ancient ulcers.

I saw him disembark
and touch land.
I only know his name:
Theseus
a boy with features of lead
and hair belonging to the night,
a boy with abstemious hands
and eyes like stained windows.

He was controlled by his destiny,
he was fasting,
his shadowy profile already fractured
in my mind.

And never had love touched me before,
never,
not even in my wildest dreams.

Today when it did
it wasn't an act of light,
it wasn't the outrageous joy
of a soaring heart,
the sanctuary of youth,
it was instead a bitter dive
into isolation,
a mute shiver of widowhood.
No, I can't – I tell myself
I can't love one who will die.
But it is already too late
and in the night,
as I lie down,
I feel that something is beginning to surrender
in my heart,
and through love,
almost imperceptibly,
I'm coming back to life.

IV
Hephaestus

I have woken up.
My hair is wet with sweat
and glued to my skin,
while throat and stomach
seem pinched by fiery pliers.
My body weighs on me:
a fabric of scars
on the compressed altar
of all the impending deaths.

Intent to assist my chaotic mind
with the foreign notion of hope,
I have got up and am now sleepwalking
towards Hephaestus' forge.

I go with my heart in a cloud of beats
and my feet covered with the dust
of a solitary road.
I walk trying not to think,
trying not to wound the sweetness
of the sky
with the swift swirl
of my terrors.

The steps are steep
and I don't know what I'm doing.

There are so many rumours about Hephaestus:
they say that He is like a naked kite
inaccessible and demonic,

that He is an outstanding blacksmith
working a high and clear anvil
on which He nails with unbending blows
all that is an obstacle to life,

that He lives like an animal
always dirty with metals and quills,
equally disdained by the man-made luxury of palaces
and by the grassy valleys of Nature,

that His body, though flawed,
is given to the ineffability
of unexplored and untiring knowledge,

that He is magnificently fierce, vindictive
and deplores with austere tension
and harsh will
all human rashness,

that He doesn't care about anything or anyone
beyond Fire
to which He gives scorpionic attention
and over which He boasts
total and precise mastery.

On reaching my destination,
touched by a despair I can hardly handle,
I see the forge
and do like the man who, on glimpsing the sea,
instead of being in awe of its immensity,
gloomily observes that he can't walk any further,
that this is the limit,
the ending point.

But Hephaestus seems to be waiting for me.
He emerges from the imperious lair
like a tongue of fire
from the mouth of the dragon
and His arcane presence
seems to blind me with a black and windy light
that divides the waters of my heart
softening with quick clarity
the solitary, unpeopled wake
of my needs,
relieving with an unexpected whisper
the bitter liquor
of my most uncertain dreams.

I am exhausted
and trembling under His turbulent gaze
I kneel down
asking with simple words
for the gift of hospitality.
I immediately feel drawn into His lair of embers
and He Himself brings me living water to drink:
a sincere, clairvoyant spurt
which irrigates my throat
thick with tears.
I feel restored, receptive, trusting.

Standing,
wrapped in pleading pride,
the cascade of my black hair
like a shady, truthful cloak,
I spell out my request:

"I want a sword or a shield
for Theseus.
I want an invincible weapon
for his fight with the Minotaur."

Hephaestus doesn't answer.
Am I asking for too much?
Asking the wrong way?
Too wilfully?
With hubris?
With scant knowledge?
I wait.
He is looking at me
and in the harsh, stagnating hum
of the increasing silence,
little by little
I lose all confidence.
Eventually I lower my eyes
unable to contain the anxiety.

At this point Hephaestus turns and disappears
into the lethargic, muscly depths
of the lair;
mysterious image of a lame,
almost human God.

I collapse to the ground,
I crouch like a stray dog.
Later, at the God's unexpected reappearance,
I weakly try to scramble to my feet.
A small, aching spot in my guts
makes me explode
into daring and intimate requests:
"Speak to me," I say to Him impetuously,
"how can I understand my destiny,

my role in this world that terrifies me
if You don't speak to me?
That's why I've come!
That's the real reason that brings me here!"
And I burst into tears
feeling exposed
I, the princess of Crete,
no longer royal
but disinherited
and in disarray.
I, the King's daughter,
reduced to hysterical heresy,
reduced to a riot of improprieties.

Hephaestus has come back holding a round object:
a sphere that glows insanely,
equation of mystery,
shadow of my rejected pain.
I stretch my hands
like a child towards a surprise:
"What is it?"
The God stares at me
upsetting with the ineffable sweetness
of a smile
all my constructions,
all my unnerved inhibitions
and at that moment I fall for Him
as for the light of the stars,
as for the divine and distant flow of the Soul.
"For Theseus" He answers
and here the flame of love is short-lived
promptly drowned
in burning disappointment
as if He had given me a loaf of charred bread
or a spoonful of bile.

"When Thetis came asking for an armour
for Achilles
You didn't give Her a ball,"
I shout full of venom,
"but I am not a Goddess like Her!
Who am I?
Nothing and nobody.
You don't pay any toll for mocking me,
for sending me back empty-handed
jeered by Heaven and Earth!"
Suddenly I take the ball out of His hands
as if I meant to smash it down
or hurl it into the fire it has come from…
except, at its touch,
something seems to soothe me
and shave my heart with a hint of consolation.
The sphere shimmers.
Impervious.
Hypnotic.
I take it to my chest.
Almost without thinking I look at Hephaestus and ask
"how can a God be lame?"
And my gaze runs to His leg
which for a fleeting, disconcerting moment
looks marked by burnings.
"You are the God of Fire," I insist,
"surely Fire cannot hurt You…?!"
The tone of my voice,
yielding to immemorial doubt,
has just forged the oblique flash
of a final question.
He seems to reproach me:
"There is an outer
and an inner Fire.
Some wounds belong to the inner Fire",

and a note of abstention
in His answer
tells me it is time to leave.
Immediately I feel my body retire
and distance itself,
but my mind lingers
still eager for explanations
about Fire,
about the ball,
about His human, wounded divinity
and in the tangle of my heart,
in the pulse of contrasting emotions
I whisper,
"Can a God be touched?"
Full of shivering impatience
and a confused, soft gratitude
I stretch my hand and brush Him lightly
with my fingertips.
Then, as I turn away,
on glimpsing His smile of cosmic parenthood
I cry out.

V
Parting

I got up in good time
before dawn stained
the leaves of the orange trees
with scents.

They didn't see me slipping out of the palace
to meet Theseus.
It was the last royal gesture
of a life lost over and over
and now become untenable.

I take Theseus by the hand.
We are on the shore of the sea
in the feverish quickening of time
and love.
He is invisible in the silvery night.
How I would like to slow down
the brightening of the sky,
to halt
the dawning roar of the Sun…

We move towards the labyrinth
like sleepwalkers absorbed by different destinies.

I want too many things from him:
that he saves himself
that he saves the others
that he loves me
that he takes me away.

I speak in bursts
through tears tripping on my lips,

through kisses crowding in
but never taking shape.
Theseus' hand, nonetheless,
squeezes mine
with persuasive and consolatory strength.
In the midst of terrors hanging over the barren,
abysmal forest
of my body,
he captures the live fabric of adventure,
the rare beat of my transformation.

It is on the vague and brutal threshold
of the labyrinth
that I entrust him the ball.
Then, on parting,
perhaps Theseus' last contact with the living world,
suddenly,
without warning,
something tender and burning erupts between us,
something draining.
We project on each other
all the love never given,
all the incompleteness of life.
We want to fill the gaps.
We want to tie to the Ideal
every contrary evidence.
Nothing stops us,
neither wisdom nor fear,
nor truth,
nor the unanswerable questions of the heart.
Finally,
in the leafing morning caressing our hair
with combs of molten gold,
in the increasing warmth,
in the silky swish of the pine groves,

Theseus ties the ball of thread to the entrance,
crosses the threshold
and is swallowed by the labyrinth
like a dead man by the Underworld.

I am left pushing my gaze into that wall
of pitch black darkness,
I'm hysterical before its sucking smoothness.

In the vortex of our parting
I believe I am being loved
and fall to my knees
screaming my prayer to the Gods.

VI
The Labyrinth

I have entered the labyrinth.
When?
Since when?
Was it an hour ago?
A month?
A year?
A lifetime?
My feet move by themselves
leading me further and further
into the dark.
I stumble forward
and slowly,
relentlessly,
I empty out.
I lose my energy drop by drop
in the effort
to understand where I'm going,
to become alive around something.
I clutch at the nothingness that surrounds me,
at the air that gets colder and colder,
I touch the walls not knowing what they are made of
while both the entrance and life
seal themselves behind me
burying me.
There's no identity here,
no form
or scope.
There's no heart to give.

Ariadne stands out in my memory
like lucid and remote music.
It feels like long ago.

Our footprints on the sand
were promptly wiped out
by the unrelenting sea.

I was watching the wind lifting her blue dress,
uncovering her ankles,
I was feeling her unripe hand
quivering in mine,
melting out of pain
and distant anger.

Oh Ariadne, I don't want to get trapped
in your vehemence
or be caught in the irreducible breath
of your love.
I want to remain warrior:
bold,
reasoning,
valiant,
free and self-contained,
committed only to the coming task.

Would my fire go out if I loved you?
Would I understand who I am if I got lost in you?
Yet I promised to take you away with me on my return,
away
to an unharmed nest,
in the wisdom of my living
and surviving,
in the obscure bereavement I will give you
by murdering your stepbrother.
Oh fragrant maiden,
the Minotaur is your brother,
you are sitting on a throne
whose fruit is contaminated

and yet you believe you can be spared?
You believe you can name your peace
and then dispense it to the people
like fine gold,
like a mouth full of honey?
Your peace is nothing but bile
in the dead heart of Greece,
in the mad spelling out
of a loser's name!
Yet I will take you away with me,
away in my boyish crush,
in the experiment they call future,
in the cauldron of all contradictions,
in my heart full of sacraments,
in my flesh of deep kisses.

What will I do with you?

I am tired of walking
listening only to my steps.
The further I venture
the more the threat of the monster floods my mind
and destroys the boy I used to be.

What will I do with you, Ariadne,
if you too flood my mind?

In the dark that gnaws at me,
in the dry echo
of this twisted box in which I'm closed,
sometimes, like a flash,
I get the idea that it's you leading me to the monster,
treacherously,
through the unravelling thread
that pulls and drags me to ruin.

Yes, with that thread
you have lured me from the cradle,
with that thread you have branded me for death,
and I,
the unaware one,
the innocent one,
I, with my barefooted heart
and cerulean mind
I have believed you as I would my own mother!
But what am I saying?
You are blameless
and you are not my mother!
It's just that darkness blots out my mind
and I no longer understand who's who:
I come down with grim confusion
and unexplored diseases!
I fear falling asleep
and I fear dreaming a beastly thunder
of male cows
and female bulls,
of half-eaten corpses
piled up in all corners
whose rigor mortis
locks all my limbs.
Oh my God
my God
I will never get out of here,
this labyrinth will be my grave!

And why, why have I come to this place?
Through which unholy folly
have I accepted the challenge
of a monster whose breath
is incendiary malevolence
and necrosis?

In order to save lives
or out of hubris?
I no longer feel the purity with which I started out,
what presses me instead,
is hunger for adulation,
the torrid arrogance
of those who pursue power.

Oh why have I come here?
To save lives or to please my father?
To feel over me the legend
of his approval,
to see the essence of his favour
blossom in my hero's heart
like divine seed?

This darkness diminishes me,
it robs me of my ideals.
Those are doors that have failed to open.
I writhe in a tangle of brier
searching inside myself
for the root of my yearnings,
for the anchor, the path to what I have lost.

Yet there is light in this grave:
Ariadne's thread unravels
with arcane shimmering.
It is milky way,
liquid, lunar reflection
that weakens or intensifies
according to the steep games
of the mind.
Perhaps it doesn't lure
but guides me,
sometimes it burns in my hands

like the fire of my youth.
There,
maybe that's why I'm here:
for my youth,
for the adventure,
the thrill of an undertaking
that's firewood on the pyre
of my holy and senseless years.
It's a homage to the ardour of muscles,
the compulsion of hormones.
Mine is the inevitable journey of someone
who doesn't know how else to find himself,
how else to look in the mirror.
Who am I?
Who am I?!
Oh if Zeus answered…
but He has abandoned me,
the Gods have abandoned me.
I have become a dead weight
on the face of the earth,
I am not even required to show the zeal,
the relief that identity brings:
what does it matter who I am in this darkness?
Who would hear me if I screamed my name
or my age?

I am the sacrificial lamb
from which no salvation will rise.

I can't help cracking up with laughter
like someone who's found out the trick
that's been played on him,
and in the vibration
of such squalid sneers
my body twists and collapses.

I slide to the ground
and I stay there.
Leaning against the wall like a beggar
I take up my last posture.
Oh yes, apathy is my new vocation.
Oh yes, I hibernate
in this liberating prison of oblivion
and I dream of the Minotaur's brutal pastimes
like an initiation to a new life.
I laugh thinking that perhaps
I too will start eating the Athenian youth,
I already feel the bites of hunger
offensive but natural.
Poor Minotaur,
what else can he do locked in here
if not eat what gets thrown at him?
He doesn't even see his meals,
he doesn't know whose instrument he is
or what aberration has generated him.
He is like the shadow
not knowing the body of which it is the image,
not knowing the sun that grants it life.
Oh unhappy monster,
our destinies fit together
and my terror flows into yours
like a river into the sea.
What will I do on meeting you?
Will I plant a knife in between your eyes
or will I cry tears of compassion?

Meantime, at my crying,
the thread has begun to shimmer more intensely,
this thread that connects me to the Soul,
that reminds me of the world,
that gives voice to the most pressing affections…

tears fall from my eyes
unexpected,
burning and unknown:
through them I surrender
to life and death alike,
through them I touch creation
and its labour,
I recognise myself.

Oh Chiron,
oh my mentor,
in this hour it is you I invoke.
Guide of my young life,
you taught me Spirit and Matter,
the military and the healing arts.
In the wonder of those days,
in the modesty
of your imperatives,
in the delicate quartz of your revelations
I forgave myself,
I took form,
never mind how many times
I questioned the bright lights of Dawn
and the pistils of the Stars,
never mind that I was always asking for more
as if your fatherly love
were never enough.

I invoke you once more, Chiron,
now, when everything unravels.
Come to give me strength.
I am ready,
I am finally ready
for the task that awaits me.

VII
Forsaken

Even now
my voice shakes at the memory.

I woke up
on the fine sands of Naxos,
close to a sea
blue with diamonds.
My body,
rested and lulled by the sound of the waves,
was opening up to freedom
and to the burning beauty
of hundreds of gorse bushes.
My hair,
dipped in seaweed,
echoed in the buzz of bees
and my heart joyously anticipated
the safe and tender touch
of love.

But an elusive silence
seemed to spread itself through the morning glow
and the farthest corner of the bay
was empty:
the ship that filled it,
the ship on which we had left Crete
was gone,
vanished!

Had coming here been only a wish,
a dream,
unripe, ephemeral fruit
of my pained and needy heart?

Where are you, my love?
When did the reins of our gallop break?
Because I no longer care for the future
my breasts have become brittle
and my face lined with the harsh creases
of premature old age.

Oh Theseus! It's as if you had told me
that I am dead.
You may have kept the thread of the labyrinth
but have thrown away that of my life!

Oh Theseus, Theseus,
how could you do this to me?
When you came out of the labyrinth
my gratitude soothed the asperity of the mountains
and the relief filled my arms to the brim.

In truth it was only my reticence that was saving me,
the respect I had for the worn-out grace
painted on your silent lips.
Indeed had I questioned you,
had I pursued the spindle of the will,
I would have pricked myself and bled to death,
I would have discovered sooner
what I was to learn later:
that you didn't love me.

You were changed,
had lost your quivering, boyish aura,
had entered a steely land
of no persuasion
and no compromise.
And I?
Did I fall in love at the wrong time?

Who were you for me if not a mirror
of the innocence I wished to recover?
Escape from cynicism,
threshold of seismic dreams,
loving absolution.
Yes, you were my absolution,
my future,
my cleansing rite.

And now I have nothing left.
No lover.
No home.
No family.
No rank.
No hope.

The beach is wetter with my tears
than with seawater.

And tell me,
tell me, you who are the one in the know,
you who believe yourself the Great Hero,
Theseus! Answer me!
What was easier
to slay the Minotaur
or to tell me the truth?

Instead you left.
Quietly.
Secretly.
Like a thief.
Oh thief of my life,
in the presence of the Gods
I cry out for vengeance!

VIII
Dionysus

Worn out by tears
and by bursts of anger,
I fell into a deep sleep
storiated with dreams.

In one I was a wild, nomadic spectator
spying on a pregnant woman
who was struck down by the beauty of the God.
I then saw Him sew her child
into His thigh
and that child emerge three months later
a dark and fleshy gift.

Alas! It is with birth that everything becomes manifold,
fragmentary,
impervious…
and while the innocent baby
was looking in a fleeting earthly mirror
for the flame of his identity,
the mighty and drab Titans
tore him to pieces
and devoured him.

Only the heart remained
and it was from the heart that the God remade Dionysus.

Oh Dionysus,
when I woke up from the dream and saw you
I saw a tall, dark youth
who was meditative and laughing,
faltering with irrevocable summers,
drunk with wine akin to Hephaestus' clairvoyant water.

Tell me, Dionysus,
what is it like to be reborn from the heart,
no longer subject to life's poisons?

Oh! In front of the inner fire
I feel the burn
of a passing identity,
of an ego dissolving into light.
Light touches me beyond self-hate,
beyond the bruised, overcast, wasted sky
of needs and memory.

Maybe in this transformation
I too will become lame?
Or maybe I shall die of ecstasy, of madness,
of the prophetic folly of Zeus
which is rebirth from the heart.

And so I walk on
guided by the dream,
guided by you
Dionysus.

CASSANDRA

Even in our sleep, pain that cannot forget
Falls drop by drop on the heart,
Until in our despair, despite us,
Comes wisdom,
By the awful grace of God.

AESCHYLUS *AGAMEMNON*

Synopsis

Cassandra is the daughter of Priam and Hecuba, King and Queen of Troy.

When still a baby she and her twin brother Helenus are left for the night in the temple of Apollo. The following morning, when Hecuba discovers them, she is disturbed to find that they are lying in the coils of two snakes sacred to the God. The snakes have licked the babies' ears opening them to the gift of prophecy.

Once grown up, Cassandra and Helenus become Apollo's priest and prophet. However, Cassandra's relationship with the God soon sours and, as she rejects him, her gift for prophecy sours too. This is clear when, no matter how much Cassandra tries to warn people against impending tragedies, nobody ever believes her.

Against the background of Cassandra's unhappiness, the fall of Troy unfolds, bloody and tragic, wanted by Gods who seem to have abandoned the city to a grim fate.

During the fall of Troy Cassandra is raped by Ajax, one of the Greek warriors. The rape happens in the temple of Athena where Cassandra has taken refuge. This makes the act sacrilegious as well as violent, unleashing the wrath of the Gods against the Greek fleet that is sailing home victorious.

Cassandra survives the sack of Troy and becomes a slave to Agamemnon, King of Mycenae and chief commander of the Greeks. Agamemnon's ship sails safely to Mycenae where he is received by his wife, Queen Clytemnestra. But ten years earlier, on leaving for the war, Agamemnon had sacrificed their daughter Iphygenia to the Gods and since her death Clytemnestra's wifely love has turned to hate.

In revenge for the death of Iphygenia she murders both Agamemnon and Cassandra.

Characters

Cassandra
Daughter of the King and Queen of Troy. She is Apollo's priestess and prophetess.

The snakes
Animals sacred to Apollo.

Apollo
God of Light and Darkness, of Healing, Music, Poetry and Prophecy.

Helenus
Cassandra's twin brother.

Hecuba
Cassandra's mother and Queen of Troy.

Priam
Cassandra's father and King of Troy.

Parthena
Cassandra's wet nurse.

Aeneas
Son of the prince Anchises and the goddess Aphrodite, he is Cassandra's cousin twice removed. He is the leader of the Dardani who are allies of the Trojans. Protected by both Aphrodite and Apollo, Aeneas will survive the war to travel to Italy and become progenitors of the Romans. He is married to Creusa whom he loses during the fall of Troy.

Aphrodite
Goddess of Love and Beauty, mother of Aeneas.

Helen
Daughter of Zeus, sister of Clytemnestra and wife of Menelaus, the King of Sparta; because of her legendary beauty she is kidnapped by Paris which triggers the Trojan War.

Paris
Cassandra's brother and Helen's kidnapper.

Hector
Cassandra's brother and heir to the throne. He is the greatest Trojan warrior. He kills Patroclus in battle and will die in a duel at the hands of Achilles who is seeking revenge for the death of Patroclus. During Patroclus' funereal rites, Achilles drags Hector's dead body behind his chariot.

Achilles
Son of the goddess Thetis and the King Peleus, he is the greatest Greek warrior.

Patroclus
Achilles' friend and lover.

Laocoön
Trojan priest and seer.

Ajax
One of the leading Greek warriors.

Athena
Goddess of Wisdom, Craft and War.

Agamemnon
King of Mycenae and chief commander of the Greek army. During the journey of the Greek fleet to Troy, Agamemnon sacrifices his own daughter Iphigenia to the Gods in order to

CASSANDRA

put an end to the lack of wind. At the end of the war Cassandra will become his slave.

Iphigenia
Agamemnon and Clytemnestra's daughter.

Clytemnestra
Queen of Mycenae and Agamemnon's wife. As soon as he comes back from the war she kills Agamemnon in revenge for the death of Iphigenia. She also kills Cassandra.

I
The Gift of Prophecy

Mute are my lips
and mute is my gaze
fixed on the waves
slapping against the hull of the ship.
Their motion makes me heavy with sleep,
fills me with an anguished weariness.

They are taking me to Greece
as a slave to Agamemnon,
I will never return to my land.

I carry my pain
as if it were a dark crow
nesting in my skin
and by night and by day
and at all hours
memory preys on me.

I was a child when Helenus and I
were left all night in Apollo's temple.
Did we get lost?
Or were we forgotten?
Or was it perhaps my mother's unconscious offering
to the God?
I only remember a feeling of shade,
of cool,
an austere relief,
passion's improvisation.
I don't recall the snakes
presences of eloquent, divine folly,
the deafening hiss of my life.

In the morning my mother found us
wide-eyed and full of sighs,
drowned in the sacred coils.
Helenus was placid,
I was in sweet spasms.
The snakes had licked our ears clean of the world's tangles,
they'd unveiled the fullness of listening,
destroyed the thin but hardy bulwark
between reason and vision,
will and advent,
between this world and the next.

Oh, I woke up to the sound of my mother's scream.
Horrified and confused
she was clapping the snakes away.
Was it this reaction that marked me
for ever?
Her implicit message
that something dangerous and inappropriate
had happened
bringing contamination to the home?
I knew then that the gift of prophecy bestowed
by the snakes
would later fester
like the pus of a shameful wound
that would re-open
and leak again and again.

Yet I wanted that gift,
I wanted it for ever
with the longing of a sunflower
turning to the light,
of a heart drunk
with love…

II
To the wolves

What do sunflowers live on?

I was a precocious child.
When lying in the golden jar
of Imagination
my hands would shake,
when Parthena lifted me out of the viscous fire
of dreams,
I would fight feebly
between ruin and salvation,
milky vision
and sharp weening.
When I got older
I used to loiter in the royal palace
wary of the luxury overflowing all around me.
Eyes fixed to the ground
I looked on the shiny floors
for the unspent coin of my half-moon face,
for the wide-open eyes of brothers and sisters
whose many names I could hardly remember.
From behind doors
I peered at those older siblings
who were blossoming
into adolescence.
I distilled from a distance
their sensual, haughty charm
that I craved for myself.
On the day of my father's birthday
we always gathered around his throne
in an anonymous,
unruly crowd
to receive a token of fatherly love,

the illusion of being raised
in a spark of sweetness.

In front of Helenus, my twin,
I felt the vertigo of the mirror
cut off from the relief of union:
he was a gentle vacuum,
the most familiar stranger I knew.

Who decided that we would both
be consecrated to Apollo?
Was it my mother's utilitarian ethics
capitalising on the gift of prophecy
or my still unconscious yet compulsive devotion?
Or was it the one God who contemplated Himself in us?
Hidden treasure searching for a heart
in which to unveil Himself
and be?

The winter of my consecration
I let myself be caught in the machinery
of the temple's affairs.
I was spellbound by the heartbeat of events,
by the obscure, alarming joy
of having found my role in life:
in the ineffable game
of ecstasy
and cruel renunciations.
Oh, but what is more beautiful
than nearing
Vocation,
Destiny?
Cost what it may.
Except it was Helenus
who was raised to the role of prophet,

as a woman I had to content myself
with the banality of ritual,
the distant and measured gestures
of priesthood.

Alas! The more I repressed them
the more the visions
surged free like sparks from an anvil.
In contrast to Helenus' simplistic collusion
with the world,
a force vibrant with accent
and pregnant with mystery
stirred in me
proclaiming with increasing impetus
the unfathomable presence of the God.

I looked for respite
in the deadening of emotions.
Torn between innocuous ceremonials
and vertiginous inner tumults,
at each weary syllable I uttered
I felt I was falling to the bottom of the sea
and, as the trance took over, a different voice
would wake me
from these subtle swoons.
I felt like a bird
lost in the blast of creation.

And so,
day after day,
delirium ploughed my soul with oracles
which, though heard by all,
remained unheeded.

Oh Phoebus Apollo,
You came to rock me in the glittering arms of Day,
You opened for me
the power of Your prophecy,
my life's potential,
an exquisite fruit,
a radiant love You had cleared of thorns.
Oh yes, at first You laid me out
on velvet,
beyond the ferocious clamour
of the living
and the procrastinating caution
of the dead,
far from the unspeakable barks
of the ignorant.
I felt fertile and unharmed,
seduced and crowned by Your authority.
Here I am, Phoebus Apollo,
I was saying,
here I am,
claim me as Your own.
I will become Your mouthpiece
in the most intimate union one could hope for…
I said yes to You
flattered and drunk
in the orbit of my ruptures,
uncertain of what I had to lose.
Maybe I believed that You would defend me,
that You would untangle the thread of my madness
and reveal it as Your most sublime handiwork.
I certainly thought I would be safe with You.
I was deluded!
I approached the Tree of Life

without realising that the roots
were poisonous tentacles!
Deluded!
You showed me one face
the instant I committed to You
and another later
when,
locked in Your totalitarian service,
too late I discovered You to be
not the God of Light
but the God who was throwing me to the wolves!

III
Insane

Defenceless,
I was thrown out into the fray
and could only try to struggle free.
Eventually the ferocity of my heart
broke the vow by which I belonged
to the God
and for ever I closed my eyes
to His sight.

I kept intruding into everybody's life.
I was hungry for goodness
yet I was spreading division
and I was living on anger.

I cannot say when I discovered
that people didn't believe me:
what I thought was Apollo's curse
took time to become
evident and sharp
the dagger of my undoing.
I ended up as a histrionic animal
spitting an incendiary panic of words.
People in the street looked at me
with derision and rancour,
with raw, terrified pity
and I couldn't work out,
I couldn't understand
what I had done
to cause this agony,
how my wish to prevent catastrophes
could turn itself
into general destitution and fracture,

the bone of contention
in the river's flood.
Was I somehow responsible
for the confusion I aroused?
Was the terror perhaps caused
by my uncompromising attitude?
The way I clung to truth?
The role of warrior
in which I discharged my reclusive passions?
The anxiety with which,
at all costs,
I was redeeming the ambiguous gift of prophecy,
trying to prove it a clear spring of knowledge
in the shapeless whirlpool
of circumstances?

I locked myself
in a thousand heroic retaliations:
"I told you so"
became my blood-letting refrain,
the obscure first-fruit I was harvesting.
Oh, my head was bursting,
my hands were shaking day and night,
even my father had abandoned me,
he wanted me locked up,
declared insane,
me, his favourite daughter!
He wanted to yank off the tooth
with which I was biting
and poisoning the kingdom.

And I *was* insane,
I *was*,
not in prophecy
but in my being rootless.

I had only wings,
wings that made me fly too high
all the way to someplace
my heart couldn't reach.

IV
Chorus

We are the witnesses.
We swing far from the funereal noose
of your words.
The sterile confusion of your oblique world
doesn't belong to us,
nor does the urgency
with which you reclaim and damn yourself.

Cassandra,
we are here
and with voice of tenderness
we want to wash your wounds.
We sit along the river
and on the water
rocking arms with wrists of reed,
turning glances like airy willows.
We write history without soaking it in tears
yet we are sensitive to the pain
by which your human destiny
plays itself out,
fades and dies away.
From us,
mute oracle,
all you can hear is a fleeting allusion
perceived in the leap
of days
and hours.
Ours is not the crowded din of predictability
but the near silence
in which you can remember how to relieve
pain.
Oh Cassandra,

it's not by the frost-bound precision
of your sleepless nights,
nor with the words
the heart fears to hear.
Instead,
let your tongue fluctuate
in sigh and doubt,
in subtle, quiet vibration.
Flee from the invasiveness
of this bitter ecstasy,
don't throw prophecy in the face of people
but let people come to you,
one by one.
You, rock of the Citadel,
harpist of tragic melodies,
attentive and private Sybil,
you must question the individual conscience
and its free will
and talk,
talk about that God
nobody understands.
Finally,
when they are ready,
speak of the ancient vehemence
that ought to be their strength,
speak of the sweet song of your senses,
give prayer with their lips
on the Scamander's banks,
do it in the hypnotic stream
of its water
by releasing the clear arrow
of your fidelity,
of the loving priesthood that seals you.

V
Aeneas

Aeneas,
in pronouncing your name
I would feel the longing
of the soul
but I would promptly repress it
by taking refuge
in a quiet, abrasive moan,
by prostrating in the temple.

Priestesses are birds in flight
that cannot pause,
they are wood shadows,
loose bitter fruits,
crystal scarred by waiting

Prophetesses are earthly sobs
lost in the incompatibility of Heavens,
they are naked ablutions
consumed by farewells.

I, priestess in the burial mound of the law,
I, incendiary prophetess,
I, cousin caught in a dream,
I am the cast effusion by which I burn,
by which, without telling the world,
I love you
Aeneas.

Our meetings were infrequent,
but every day,

with closed eyes and taut heart,
I would catch sight of you
moving in the noise of the city
or standing as a silhouette
against the patriotic beauty
of the Citadel.
Your steels inhabited me
like mute, sharp visions,
like a male soliloquy.
Your gaze calmed my spirit
with the chimes of tall beeches.
Oh Aeneas,
in you there's inner gentleness
and peace,
infinite magnanimity
and compassion,
as for the touch of your hand,
it was for me
like radiant dew,
a tangible and safe shore
that my body could renounce if it must
but my essence could not,
nor could the generous eternity
on my lips
or the starting heart
hidden in lowered eyelashes.

*Priestesses are reluctant stags
in the fecundity of the sacred,
are nomadic lionesses of ancient courage.*

*Prophetesses are incandescent cinders
in the extravagance of voices*

and I, Aeneas,
I am for ever the one who stands by you
with the tender breath
and tension
of my short life.

VI
Last Meeting

Aeneas,
you came to the temple
to see me
when the city was about to fall.

There was no formality,
no delay
or alternative.

I saw you from afar
in the heartbeat of fidelity
and in my wait
I was lighting a candle
to the darkness of the Soul,
I was feeding the brooks of my farewells
and loosening my long hair to the fury
of the wind,
I was crying
with fingers consumed by desire,
with wide open eyes
that had contemplated
the destruction of the city,
the abortion of Proverbs,
the ruinous call
of Dawn.

We stood on the inner steps
of the temple
as if floating in dreams,
and in the pressing spasm
of Time
I would have kissed your hand

bringing you
not the breaking of taboos
but the shy splendour
of my devotion.
I couldn't do it
paralysed by permissions
I had never asked for,
suspended in the fog of non-existence.
"Come to my aid,"
whispered my painful rhymes.
"I won't collapse, I am strong,"
answered the windows of the Soul.

I spoke like a flooding torrent:
    "Troy is finished.
    Our homeland is fading away.
    The cloth of the ancestors is being undone.
    If you
    you alone, Aeneas, believe me
    it's enough for me.
    I won't ask for more,
    I'll die at peace.
    Oh, you will not die,
    you have a mission to accomplish.
    You will survive
    the black fire of the crows,
    the disgust of the Gods,
    the stray sins
    of those who've started this carnage
    not for Helen's exquisite, hard
    face
    but for a drunken brotherhood
    with the Underworld,
    out of sheer greed.

This is my voice
that steps into the limbo of the sacred,
disdains the weakness of ritual
and doesn't fear the discipline
of the righteous.

Oh, how can it be
that Troy,
Queen of Anatolia,
cosmopolitan orchard,
filigree of grace and scents,
temple of silk and thunder,
treasure chest of youth and ardour,
anchor of our illusions,
barn of history,
lyre distilled in the bell of all heroes,
how can it be that Troy
closes her eyes for ever,
lies in the sobless grave
of Nothingness,
in the boredom of fossilised dogs,
in the hideous crockery
the future will excavate
with abortive archaeology!
Oh unhappy Trojans,
I see first
the crackling mouth of fire,
then the Earth which will suffocate us
without mercy
and with no respect
for the solitary
or the gregarious,
for the one who is seeking vengeance
or the one who is nothing but a peaceful pilgrim
along the branches of the cedar.

People of Troy,
do not cover your eyes with planks,
do not close your ears with cork
but let the prophets teach you
how to prune the knotty shrub
of your ego,
how to walk in the coils
of farewell.
This I tell you
but it is wasted breath
because humans
don't know their own good!"

Oh Aeneas,
how long did you stay with me?

When you took my hand
and gently asked
if it had been Apollo turning His back on me
or me turning mine on Him,
my body became tense
and the heart skipped a beat
out of anger and anguish.

I felt misunderstood, accused.

    "You were too young for all this." you said,
    "your candle burned too fast:
    thrown to the vast, unknown land
    of the sacred,
    overwhelmed by the extreme demands
    of your ungovernable talents
    you went on without a guide
    except that of your passionate ignorance.
    What do you know of the Gods?

What do you know of Apollo?
Have you heard His music?
His ineffable poetry?
How many times have you been in His dark, healing caves
seeking the oracle of dreams?
Have you touched the vertigo
of footsteps
in the chambers of the heart?
Were you so frightened
as to take flight
from the Experience?
Yet I see light in you,
light that doesn't crumble or fade.
Cassandra, I want you to sustain that light
because we will all need it
when the time comes.
Oh yes, I believe you,
our destiny *is* marked,
Aphrodite points to me the future.
I am not privy
to the why
or how
or when:
as soon as I ask
She ignores me, Her son,
the way She would a common mortal,
nonetheless I know
that we will be swept away
by the inflexible logic of History
and our vanishing
will be like the scattering of dust,
like the mysterious turning of the doors
of Time,
like the breath
of transiting seasons."

Aeneas,
you touched my hair
and with a face stained with tears
saw my stupor,
the raging confusion
of my feelings,
my anxiously drinking the intimacy
of your emotions.
As our consciousness exploded
you kept talking as if a dam had opened in your heart:

    "Don't ever separate your pain
    from your tenderness,
    remain celestial
    and warlike
    like you were when Apollo chose you
    to remind us,
    in all this folly,
    of the light footsteps
    of sanity."

"Light? Sanity?" I stammered,
hearing in my skull
the hiss of the snakes,
the dreadful off-beat sound
of Hecuba's hands driving them away,
the running water of my holocaust;
and in the eternity of that instant,
in the yearning for my own Self,
in your moving away from me,
I felt I could gaze at the Sun
and know both
Order
and Chaos
Certainty
and Regret.

VII
Like a Shadow

I don't want to understand.
I don't want to remember.
The journey on this ship is my only rest,
I've been granted a moment of limbo
between two hells
why poison it
day and night
with memories?
As if compulsive reminiscing
could give birth to a different life,
generate a less painful narrative.
It doesn't work like that.
The images come
like a red hot vortex,
definitive scenarios,
grotesque theatres
I will never be able to leave.

After Priam, I was the first
to see Hector dead,
his body a disfigured lump of flesh.
I knew it wasn't the ordinary hatred
of war
but Achilles' personal vendetta
for the death
of Patroclus.
It was the homicidal fury
of pain,
of loss,
of love that doesn't know its source,
of life that loses its meaning.

I caught sight of my father,
aged from one day to the next,
dragging himself away,
his knees still dirty with the mud
in which he had knelt
imploring for the remains of his son.

And I?
I was like a shadow
lost in the vastness of military camps,
lost in the vastness of existence,
Trojan?
Greek?
Who was I then?
Who am I now?
What does it matter?
All we've got left is tears.

VIII
Troy

First Movement

Memory never gives respite.
Now, in the procession of nightmares,
the gates of the city
are flung wide open
and the Horse makes its way in
pulled by thousands of hands:
the ropes groaning,
the backs sweating,
the sinister squeak of wheels,
the distant thunder
of its deadly belly…

The Horse is gigantic,
dark,
a hallucinatory shadow
fashioned from the very timber of which coffins are made.
Thanks to what sermons,
due to which ancient violation
has it infiltrated
our minds,
our bodies?
Don't make me see it!
Oh cruel mind,
don't present me again with that vision
of an atrocious toy.
How was it possible that years of heroism
should end like this,
in the treacherous swamp of its shadow,
in the secret and obscene roar
of its flanks?

When I saw it standing tall
within the walls of the city
I lost it
and with axe in hand
I ran down from the Citadel
like a maniac
wanting to throw myself against its limbs,
those monstrous, tenacious towers
that were crushing mother Earth
hell-bent on sucking out
all its lifeblood.

And yet, and yet
the fury animating me
felt suddenly more like self-hate,
it was as if the axe moved by itself
and hit not the Horse
but what was left
of my Soul...
it tried to destroy at a single stroke
the source of prophecy,
unredeemed balm of my life.

I wasn't the only one
to hit the Horse:
Old Laocoön hurled
a spear
against its sleek,
treacherous curves.
The iron burnt the air over my head
before planting itself
in the underbelly
of the monster
which echoed with the cavernous sound

of inscrutable sewers.
Alas! No sooner had the spear
stopped vibrating
than two huge snakes
crawled out of the sea
and, coiling around Laocoön,
crushed him to death.
The horror of that vision
still stalks my mind.
As in a dream
I saw two innocent children lost in the temple,
trusting and easy
in the embrace of sweet, forked tongues,
and felt confused terror
at the incomprehensible asperity
of such sweetness.
"No! No! No!"
I shouted at the top of my voice
but I could hardly hear myself
as if speaking from
a great distance.
I passed out
as a thousand arms took hold of me,
wrenched the axe from my hand
and dragged me in the dust.

Second Movement

In the twisted crease
of her young nights,
when Priam still assaulted her
with greedy kisses
and children kept multiplying
in her womb,
when she was pregnant with

Paris,
my mother dreamt of a blazing torch
alive with snakes
and she read in the heart of the dream
Fate's awful choice:
that this unborn son
would one day cause Troy's ruin.

And so my mother
knelt on a stone floor
and tore from her chest
all the waves of the river.
She said to the shepherd:

"You must kill my son for me.
You will do it with toys armed with fog."

Yet in my dark perception
I knew that my brother had survived.
Through the all-seeing eye
I learnt that one day he would come back
and carry into the kernel
of destiny
the careless touch
of his sweet, twisted beauty,
the trivial infamy
of his mind.

Dragged into the heart
of the Citadel
where my father would usually have me locked,
the Horse secure within the city walls,
I contemplated the horror of the moment.
I had a clear vision

of Hecuba's dream
and of everything that was coming to pass.

Where was my father?
I screamed with filial despair,
I threw myself against the walls of my cell,
limbs scratched by the Gods.
I let the trance I drank
drown me in pain and fire
until the veil of dusk
fell on my exhausted brow
and I heard the door of the cell being unlocked.
In the foreboding silence
not yet echoing with death,
for an instant,
I sensed
the indecipherable presence
of my father.
Yet I could not turn to him
not with thoughts,
nor with sounds.
Inarticulate and spent
I lay alone in the shuttle of the hours.

I felt the hawthorn burn,
saw the coruscating light of the flames climb walls,
heard the clanging of arms,
I saw the sons and the daughters
of my land
fall like a rain of stones and ghosts
driven by a passion devoid of mercy.
I could no longer care for myself
and when I bolted from the cell
towards the temple,

any temple,
it was no longer me running
but someone moving and acting in my place,
someone gathering everything with violent love
and saving it for ever
in a heart bigger than the Universe,
in a heart like the dome
of the sky.
Is it possible to become so vast?
Is it possible,
in the depth of despair,
to become a sanctuary for the whole world?
Is it possible?

It was Ajax who found me.
He raped me in Athena's temple
where I had taken refuge.
As I clung to the wooden statue
of the Goddess,
I found such strength as to unhinge it.
I invoked Athena's help
mouth full of thorns,
hands made of nails
and my mind
a sword harder and sharper
than diamond,
more penetrating
than the phallus of any man.

Oh Ajax,
your sacrilege was drenched in death,
a damnation for the whole of Greece.
Too late to save Troy,
nonetheless such violence and profanation
marked the turning of the tide,

and when the wrath of the Gods
fell on the Greek fleet returning Home,
it was clear that,
indirectly,
I had done more harm to the enemy
than all the Trojans in ten years
of war.
Did I rejoice?
Was it justice?
What is justice if not the hand that levels
winners and losers?

IX
Night

Mute are my lips
and mute is my gaze
fixed on the waves
which lap the hull of the ship.
My memory is
a double-edged blade,
a distant razor
cutting its way into my nights,
filling with heartbreak
the macabre eye of the sky.

Sometimes Agamemnon appears before me
like a shadow,
a distortion.
He is dreamlike and yet alive,
arrogant and foreboding,
lost in the slow annunciation
of a future of blood he cannot fathom.
He looks at me.
I see him
inert ghost,
dead victor.
He unconsciously trembles to the toll
of the bells of Destiny.
He doesn't dare violate me,
doesn't dare touch me:
I intimidate him,
I scare him,
I can read in his face
the uncertainty contaminating him:
after years of war
he no longer knows himself.

He no longer knows this man who lives inside him
and who is now heading for home,
he no longer knows what home is,
falters before the domestic mysteries
in wait.
He doesn't know with what gestures
to thaw a marriage that used to be
crack of hunger
and flame of lamps.
He doesn't know
what Clytemnestra's slate eyes will say,
but I do.
They will say:

"My husband?
I didn't know that war fattened people.
I endured the beast of your absence.
I endured…what for a mother is the unspeakable.
Vulgarity is painless.
Brutality is infectious.
A plot? Since when?
Killing diminishes boredom.
Regicide quenches rage.
Time erodes the heart.
Everything passes.
Everything ends.
Nothing goes back to what it was."

Oh, it's the dead of night,
he can't sleep,
I can't either.
He is drawn to the corner where I crouch.
He gets close and almost brushes my hand.
Agamemnon.
A moan escapes his chin,

a grunt obstructs his mind
but Iphigenia is dead,
dead for ever
like all dead that no century to come can wake.
He comes closer and almost brushes my hand
like a plea for atonement.
I don't shrink from him.
I could laugh in his face,
whip him with the bloody visions
dripping all around me,
or I could say:
"Let's change course,
let's learn to live,
to save ourselves,
our mummified lives
maybe still have a meaning."
I don't do either thing.
Idle in the longevity of renunciation,
certain of the futility of my games,
I wink at Apollo and mumble:
"What will You do if I shut up?
If I don't prophesy any more?
If I don't even ever speak again?
If I don't give You the satisfaction?"

And my heart breaks.

X
Chorus

Oh Cassandra,
flower cut in the winter of the Universe,
if we could grant you a different journey
on this desolate ship
we would do that,
but we don't have the power
to turn you from the deadly destiny
the prow ceaselessly opens.
Alone,
in the silence of days,
in the surging rigour of the waves,
in the remorse of the wind,
in the antagonism of all petitions,
in the absence of mediation,
remember
that you are still sacred to Apollo,
remember
that He is still as close to you
as your skin.

He has placed inside you
what you sought outside,
the radiance in which you knew Him,
the love He had cleared of all thorns.

*Oh, what you are looking for is not in the world,
it is inside yourself.*

Ask Him to explain the sunny shade
of that place
with a lover's patience.

Ask Him to lift the opaque veils
of your dissent
and terror,
one by one,
all summer long,
in tender scrambles
and thirsty embraces.
Ask Him to reveal the vision
in which one day
you may gather yourself again
and be renewed.

XI
The Atom of Silence

What is left?
What should we talk about?
When the atom of silence melts and impregnates the world
even breath surrenders,
there's no blowing of air all about,
no shadow to circle the Soul,
even the seawater pours from the brim of its crests
without motion,
without ablution,
without the subtle pattering
of distraction,
without scars.

I, Cassandra,
hear whispers and voices:
the intimate, dancing chorus
of wisdom and stillness.

I feel the need to unlearn everything,
I feel this longing in my heart
for all that is hidden.
I can no longer say no
and I can no longer say yes
but an infinite bewilderment has taken hold of me
and now,
now that with dawn the ship enters the harbour,
there is one question,
only one question tormenting me:

Am I still in time?
Am I still in time?

PSYCHE

And all shall be well and
All manner of thing shall be well
By the purification of the motive
In the ground of our beseeching.

T. S. ELIOT

Synopsis

There was a King who had three daughters. The youngest, Psyche, was so beautiful she looked like a goddess. Her fame had spread so far that there was a constant stream of people coming to the royal palace to admire her. In time people started to say that she was even more beautiful than Aphrodite and turned to worshipping her instead of the Goddess.

Psyche, however, was sad and lonely because nobody ever fell in love with her. Men would come and go daunted by her beauty. She and her family feared she would never marry.

Her distressed father went to see the oracle of Delphi to ask Apollo for advice. The answer was terrible: Psyche was supposed to be led to the top of a hill and left there alone. A winged serpent would come and take her as his bride.

Psyche prepared for this marriage as for a funeral and was abandoned on the hill by family and friends who wept for her fate: a fate they couldn't change.

Psyche sat on the spot, mute and terrified, until the soft wind of Zephyr came and gently blew her off the hill all the way to a verdant meadow overlooked by a beautiful castle.

Psyche entered the castle and slowly took possession of it. She started spending her days in luxury and her nights in the arms of a mysterious, loving man who filled her with joy but whom she was forbidden to see. Initially she accepted the prohibition. She was so happy she didn't mind meeting her husband in darkness and being denied the chance to see his face. However, when her two sisters came to visit, they sowed the seeds of doubt in her. They insinuated that her husband was no other than the disgusting, evil, winged snake of the prophecy: no wonder he didn't want to be seen.

From that day on Psyche lost her peace. Her sisters must be right, surely no one would behave like her husband unless he had something terrible to hide. After many days of inner agony,

Psyche finally decided to wait until her husband was asleep, then she would approach him with a candle and find out the truth.

The light didn't show a monster but Eros the God of love – the most beautiful creature imaginable. Psyche fell to her knees awash with relief and gratitude, but in her happiness she shook the candle and a drop of hot wax fell on Eros' naked shoulder. The God woke in pain and, realising Psyche's disobedience, was furious. He left her.

Psyche spent a long time in utter despair and bewilderment until she decided to face Aphrodite who, being both Eros' mother and her rival in beauty, was presumably the source of all her troubles.

Aphrodite hinted at the fact that Psyche might one day see Eros again provided she passed a series of tests.

Psyche found enough strength, guidance and help to pass the first three but the last one proved to be the hardest. She was asked to visit the Kingdom of the Dead and collect a gift from Persephone to Aphrodite. The gift was sitting in a small casket which Psyche was not supposed to open under any circumstances. Unfortunately Psyche's feeling of inadequacy and her need to know were once again too strong to control and she opened the casket both to see what the gift was and to partake of it. As she lifted the lid, a fatal cloud of poison was unleashed. Psyche was instantly overwhelmed and soon found herself close to death. Eros, however, had been watching over her. He promptly intervened and revived her by dispersing the poison gas with the fanning motion of His wings.

Psyche was saved and her happiness restored. The Gods allowed Eros and Psyche to marry and they lived happily ever after on Mount Olympus.

Characters

Psyche
A princess.

Eros
God of love.

Aphrodite
Goddess of love.

Zeus
King of all Gods.

Icarus
He was the son of Daedalus who created the labyrinth where the Minotaur lived. Daedalus and Icarus tried to escape from Crete using wings made of feathers and wax but Icarus flew too near the sun and his wings melted. He fell to his death.

Charon
He carries the Souls of the newly dead across the river Styx into the Underworld.

The Fates
The three Goddesses of destiny. They assign to every human his or her fate according to the counsel of the Gods. Klotho spins the thread of life, Lachesis measures it and Atropos cuts it.

Cerberus
A three-headed dog guarding the gates of the Underworld.

Persephone
Queen of the Underworld.

I
Spell

I was wandering in a world
of mirrors,
of gardens full of symmetrical glamour,
a harmony without remedy,
allusive,
would sometimes besiege my spirit,
empty my voice
of any tone.

I would squander my days
feeling guilty for everything:
for being beautiful,
for being a woman,
for being alive.
I was unable to bear
the changes in my fortune:
the blows that destiny was dealing me,
the sourness of a life
walked on paths
I hadn't chosen.

Beauty,
oh beauty,
you transfigured my face.
Men whispered about me
in the inflamed bastion
of desire.
They would come to see
and worship me
like a goddess
but then they would disappear
as daunted pilgrims.

In my confusion
I only remember my father's
verdict
which gave me no hope:

"Maiden of blinding beauty,"
my father said:
"exposed and unconscious peak,
long is your journey Home,
too long for the constancy and daring
of lovers,
you will never marry
and what will we do with you?"

The face of Day terrified me,
The music of the Night
wounded my sex
and I knew nothing of the heart.

In the end I don't know what was worst:
the Oracle's intimation
that I would marry a winged snake
or everybody's abandonment
when I was finally exposed
to such destiny
and, obliterated by History,
taken onto the hill to wait
for the monster.

I waited for him
hands joined together,
speechless,
dry-eyed,
locked in my tortured mind,
a mind already faltering,

a mind whose seed of madness is still sprouting
among my innermost thoughts.

Oh Zephyr, merciful Zephyr,
by your divine breath
I was saved:
you blew me away from the hill
to where there was still hope
for less ferocious encounters
and for a life worth living.
You took me to a green valley
and a mysterious, silent palace.
There I was allowed a supreme,
most pure joy:
one love almost too great.

My lover comes to me every night.
He visits me with velvety voice
and oiled, handsome body
made of muscles like faceted diamonds.
I don't know who he is,
I must not see him
and I shouldn't even speak of him,
so this description, alas,
already breaks the vow.
Indeed in our meetings
darkness fully envelops us
as vast as a forest,
as deep as a sweet abyss.
It guards the mystery
and vanquishes the wearing hammering
of Reason,
relegates drunken me to a place
I do not understand.

Oh, but what do I care if I don't know who he is,
what do I care if I can't see him
as long as my fingers can plunge through his
almond hair
and I can hear the heart beat in the labyrinths
of his chest?
Who is he?
Who is my lover?
They say he is a God,
a piece of gossip
as sharp as my irreverent boasting:
"Ha! Don't you know?
My man is a dweller of Olympus!
What a catch!"
Modesty, modesty, grandmother used to admonish,
but how can I be modest,
me, a mortal, ordinary girl,
me loved by a God?
I can't get my head round it,
me reconnected to the Splendour
of the Universe
by a tenderness that heals all denials?

Oh, at night only do I want to live
when he approaches the palace
and the rooms come alive in my mind
one by one
like candles lighting up.
I wait for him hands joined together
like I did for the winged snake
and in the fantastic wake
of his arrival
my knees bend on the wedding bed
like those of a fawn
hypnotised by the whispering wind.

Do not tell me I must leave,
flee from him
because I can't see his face,
because in the darkness I might mistakenly kiss
a monster treacherously solidified at my feet.
Do not tell me
that the velvet of his skin is deceptive
and that if my hand lingered
long enough
it would turn cold and scaly
like that of a reptile.
No, do not tell me that his wings
(indeed he has wings!)
are too much of a coincidence
for him not to embody
a prophecy
which, once pronounced,
thumps the Universe with fast hooves
eager to reach without delay
its unwitting recipient.

I'm exhausted, sisters,
you come to visit only to fuel my
doubts,
to drain me
with your poisonous orations.
I am so tired of doubting
that I often fall into his arms
like a dead weight
and he doesn't know what to do with me:
whether to let me rest
or to instruct with his male energy
every molecule of my pliable,
sleepy body…
or is it my mind which is sleepy?

Is it?
Tell me if the seed of madness
stirs
awoken by too much happiness.
It is an inner force
bent on destruction,
determined to repeat the past
and never let happiness settle
in my life.
Because happiness is a foreign body,
a fistful of dust in the eyes,
a garment far too garish
to be worn by mortal.
It is not becoming!

Days and nights
I ask the reason
for his concealment.
Why doesn't he want me to see him
if he's got nothing to hide?
Don't I have the right
to contemplate the face
of the man I touch?
I want all or nothing.
Why this half-baked, nonsensical thing
made of menacing darkness
and grim,
lopsided thoughts
that spoil the precarious joy
of the heart?
Surely if he loves me
he will be able to hold
the forays of my gaze,
he will know how to surrender
to my loving pupils,

how to melt in the annals of my irises,
and wouldn't he himself want to rest his ardent eyes
over my candid breasts,
see the radiant beauty
of my young body,
subtle veil,
steep husk
of a yearning soul?

It is a fact
that at each encounter
I pull further away from him
troubled as I am by this situation
which is becoming unsustainable.

Recently I entertained the idea
of his possible double nature:
half God
half Beast.
Maybe he flees from me at the stroke
of the Metamorphosis,
of his shapeshifting into
teeth,
coils,
reptilian, demonic wings…

He lies to me!
He lies!
But what bothers me the most
is having to walk on the sharp blade
of uncertainty.
My feet bleed from it.
In vain,
at times,
a voice inside me

screams that such blood might be blessed and essential,
that uncertainty is salt of the earth,
the teaching by which the incarnating Soul
clothes herself,
and if I dwell with Divinity
to It I must surrender all my security.
Outside,
outside the obstinate shell
of a controlling ego
who wants all easy and clear
there are spheres more ineffable than the Sun
whose disc Apollo raises in the sky
with daily, untiring
motion.

Oh! Wise words
but it's too late:
my brow has turned resolute,
warlike,
I will fight for my love,
I will get rid of the obnoxious obstacle
without risk
or prayer.

I know what to do:
I will wait for my beloved to fall asleep,
then,
bent over him,
I will pierce darkness and all its secrets
by peering in discreet candle light
at his face
suffused with dreams.

I have decided to act.
Oh! What a daunting, frightful moment,

pure trembling exultation!
As I get close with the flame
I believe myself born again,
the equal of Prometheus who stole the fire
from the Gods.
After so much torment
I am brandishing my payback time,
throbbing, injurious payback.
I am showing Olympus
how one chooses the best,
how one reacts to life's neglect
and the fatalities of the journey.
I
I decide.
I, the one who wants the God
not the winged snake.
I, who in the chessboard game of my breathing life
professes one and not the other.
I, the one who wants to empty her limbs
of the litany of pain
and pass to her children
a single most sweet rhyme:
the rhyme of
JOY!

Never was candle more furtive
yet impudent,
never was candle more thirsty for fire
and free will.
The flame
breaks darkness,
turns itself into creator,
into the dispenser of a most sweet surprise:
oh yes, what I see is the most beautiful face
imaginable,

I can barely resist the impulse
to stretch my hand
and touch its terse profile
while a wave of relief
as immense as the sea
washes over me.

I am a thief,
a thief of visions!
And I fall to my knees
singing my gratitude,
singing a new dawn
of certainty,
peace
and harmony.

Alas! In the jumble of emotions
I shake the candle
and a drop of hot wax
falls on the naked shoulder
of the one I now know to be
none but Eros,
the God of Love!

He wakes up!
I jump to my feet with a cry
which is already a plea!
I expect a chance to talk,
to ask for forgiveness,
to trustingly turn to Him
even in the moment
of disobedience,
but the anger in His eyes,
the desolation on His lips
are inextinguishable:

a sky permanently torn asunder
by lightning,
a world fixed for ever in that hard,
distorting flash,
my otherness,
my ephemeral, mortal substance
definitively exposed
and judged.
His rage pierces me
with a pain steeped in nostalgia.
It penetrates my body
unleashing a carnal desire
which clings to my limbs
like a poisoned cocoon
and from that moment on
the litany of the days I must live without Him
starts to spool itself out:
a slow rosary
of inner death,
of absence of all meaning
and desires,
of absence of anything
that is alive and breathing.

II
Loss

I don't want to get up
from this famished pallet.
Wide-eyed,
motionless,
I pass my days
as in a coma.

Only by night
do I stir
to rub my hands on stones,
to pee on moon leaves.

When I feel dizzy
and my mouth
vomits
I think:
"I should have approached Him with the knife
not with the candle,
with the knife!"
But to what purpose?

I refuse to surrender
to the stench of experience
and I laugh at my folly
which wanted to change destinies marked
by the malevolence
of the Gods,
marked by human inadequacy.

His hand in my hair
was tender immersion.
The pure spark

of His profile
was a loveliness
seen only once
in a lifetime.
How can I teach my body rest?
How can I teach it
the indifferent postures of muted living
when no love language is inscribed
in the living flesh
and skin
and limbs
are vocation to exile?
Ah, the heart is unable
to leave that room
where love seemed true
and lasting!
Alas! the bud in the womb
was nothing but an aborted foetus!

I eat the clods of the earth,
drink the semen of Your orgasms,
lift the unknown sore
like the hem of a dress,
see in the mirror
my face distorted by the flood.

I can no longer tell
what I had
from what I hoped to have,
what I used to miss
from what I still miss,
what I have lost
from what is left.

III
Once upon a time

Once upon a time
there was a Man
who almost looked like a Boy,
naked,
with wings as blanched as wax,
much cleverer than Icarus'.
Wherever He went He destroyed
the Day
in order to create
a mendacious Night.
He let Himself be explored
by my fingers as by lilies and anemones
but when the roses started
to burn
and my pupils made their way
to His Soul,
then He faded,
He shortened like an indecent snail
poked back into the shell.
Suddenly He was no longer speaking
of closeness,
of abandon,
but a carnival of obscene admonishments
dripped from His brow
pressing me.
Do I remember well
or am I making it all up?
Has the pain
perhaps
chopped off the flow of memory?
Eros, isn't it true
that You didn't want to be known,

that at the first sign
of true intimacy
You ran to your mother, Aphrodite,
like a schoolboy addicted to Her nod?
She has always hated me
because the suitors,
sumptuously dazzled by my rival
beauty
and presumed divinity,
would sacrifice to me
and not to Her.

Who punishes
who is punished
on the road to Knowledge?

IV
Who is this Woman?

Who is this Woman
who marches through the North
of my loss?
Have I ever seen
the firm authority
of Her shoulder,
the all-embracing,
savage curl
of Her locks,
the eclipsing pupil
of Her disdain,
the mothering well
of Her nipples?
Have I ever guessed
at the ageless
bloom
of Her shroud?

I will wear out
the fictitious doll
with the sound of my despair.
I will go to the source of my trouble,
I will bring the plague
right on Her doorstep!
I will howl from the pit of my throat
until She hears.
I will munch my grit
and spit my fire.
I will hang on Her braid
like the daughter of
doomsday!

Or maybe, maybe
I will plead my way
into Her dreamy
eye,
into the shadowy power
of the sea
She emerged from.

Oh! I'm not the eternal sufferer,
the defeated maid
made of illusions!
I will crawl out of my
morgue
and interrogate the Goddess.
I will answer back,
I will scream at Aphrodite,
I will deny Her
my destiny!

V
Form

Is Aphrodite my destiny?

Standing before the blank crease
of Her mouth,
swimming in the cold star
of Her eyes
I see darkness rise.

I hear the words
of the Goddess
like otherworldly vapours,
they command me to show Her
my worth,
to redeem my wedding gown.

I don't understand
is She putting me to the test?

Aphrodite shows me
a solid dune of seeds
that is as vast as the desert,
as high as the space between my shadow
and the sun.
She says I must separate and order the seeds
by dawn,
each and every one of them,
as many and different as they are!

This is not possible.
I will never make it.
I'm keeling over.

I want to die.
Since Eros abandoned me
I've never stopped wishing for death.

But this is the task.

Night gathers.
I sit beside the seeds –
diseased food,
incestuous vision,
projection of my confusion.
Confused…
that's how I felt when I thrashed about
insane with love
and doubt,
lost to annunciations,
bound by fog,
dominated and deformed
by an intermittent God,
uncertain of what to embrace
whether His body
or my consciousness.

And now I sit petrified.
I don't know what to do any more.
Until in the angular, lunar pallor,
in the glassy silence,
a humble ant
comes forward
and promises help.

"We will order the seeds for you,"
she announces
while shaking a head

tinier than any seed:
a dark,
surreal dot
in the stain of Time.

As if by miracle
ten thousand ants surge:
a dark eclipse,
a teeming,
industrious carpet of insects.
I look at them order
the seeds.
They work like my hands,
run like my feet,
clutch like my teeth.
Oh yes, this is the miracle,
my unique, exquisite
miracle!

The sun already replaces the moon,
dissolves it
in the orange dawn.

I experience the clarity
of Separation,
of Form,
of Discernment,
play of a geometry
which denounces Idols
and digests the Night,
which defines Space
and coagulates the World.

For the first time ever
I feel surprise,
I feel the leap of the heart
at my identity,
at the sound
of my ancient name:
Psyche.

VI
Power

Oh these tasks!
They are like the tide,
they are what rushes forth
and what retreats,
the fullness and the emptiness
of my body.
Each time I face them
staggering in the dark hum
of my bruises,
invoking my innocence
or impunity,
negotiating the desolate land
of the heart,
facing the implacable Goddess
who is my tombstone
and my delirious fever.

Yet when night falls
I dream of another
Aphrodite:
lovingly dishevelled,
shining with sweet whispers.
Her cupped, suffering hands
offer me the tasks
like favours the Soul accepts with reverence:
a masculine bread that makes me
more womanly.

For my second task
Aphrodite commands me
to gather the golden wool

of the rams that graze
beyond the river:
the Sun rams,
terrible animals
that are more violent than bulls.
Alas! I fear they will destroy
my body
with their secular bellowing
and, merciless, will drink
my Soul
by pouring it down the spur of their
throats.

I walk along the river.
It is glittering with blood
and shadow.
I burn with terror
and with greediness
for those precious fleeces.

How will I accomplish this task?
What will become of me?

Desperate, I enter the water
to quench the fire in the heart,
to drown myself,
to get it over and done with!
But here, on the bank,
unexpectedly,
the reeds,
so green and divine,
start whispering to me
healing litanies
that soothe my tears.

To succeed in this task,
the reeds say,
I will have to act at sunset.
When the rams,
after spending the solar energy
of their demented horns,
retreat to the soft gleaming of twilight,
I must squat on the margins
of their cosmic pen.
I must avoid those furious snouts,
give a wide berth
to their flaming bowels,
flee the belligerent slit
in their irises.
When the sun goes down
I must wait till they gather
in the increasing physicality,
in the abyss without memory
that guides them.
Hidden under their Earth,
with the sighing hand
of a thief,
I must grab only the clumps
of their fleece
left entangled in the bushes.

Those clumps
are abrasions on the thirsty crust
of the Earth,
male, solar detritus,
golden anchor to my need.
I will grasp them
with avid horror,
I will pile them up

in my basket
mindful
of their blinding, sensual touch,
careful not to take
more than I need.
If I don't burn out with desire
or terror,
if I survive,
then I will throw my loot
at Aphrodite's feet.
In the final agony of the night
She will tell me
if my sacrifice and my restraint are enough,
if this time I have finally paid
my debt.

VII
Learning

The infernal river of my mind
burns timelessly
in the landscape of Death,
it is mirrored and embodied
by the outer waters I have to face:
the Hell inside
and the Hell outside.

I sit breathless and still
in the silent groan of my days.
Each day speaks the harsh words
of a new trial.
This is the third.
There will be more and more:
I feel Aphrodite won't give me a break
until I'm destroyed!

Oh! A mountain looms over me,
a rock shows me my destiny,
spits from its fleshless
jaws
the repulsive, black
water
I never wanted to see,
water that roars,
water shamelessly drunk by the sins of the world.
Oh yes, this is the river Styx.
I have walked for days to meet it.
It is black,
circular
like a snake eating its tail,
like a scorpion in the asshole!

Aphrodite wants Her crystal goblet
filled with its water
and I'm the one
condemned to fill it for Her.
Ha! I can't even get near:
dragons with metal eyes
and rapacious scales
slide in the treacherous
marsh
of the banks,
if I make one step
I slip on the slimy stones,
I plummet in the abyss
separating the Living
from the Dead.

Who is alive?
Who is dead?
Where
where did the Gods place
the border?
Where does
making
begin to turn into
unmaking?
How can I avert my thoughts
from the brevity of things
that so oppresses me,
that so confuses my hand
naturally stretched towards
the eternal?
And why wasn't I supposed to look
at Eros?
What was wrong with that?
In the vast climax of things

was it a sin trying to find out
who He was,
who we were?
Was it a sin
wanting to drink from the fountain
of my youth?
Wanting to absorb and live life
to the full?

The Styx is Life.
The Styx is Death.
The Styx is crucible of the world.
And my empty goblet
will remain empty,
this delicate vessel that could only break
in the sinister, crashing
waves…

But while my eyes
begin to close
made vague
in the fog of renunciation,
suddenly here it is:
Zeus' eagle!
It flies across the sky
tearing it apart with its sure claw.
It looms over me.
It fills the sky
like a newly born God!
And I,
between fright and surprise,
I feel the unashamed
urge
to learn if my salvation,
this time,

could truly come from such Heights.
I feel dizzy following the revolutions
of the bird
and when I meet
its peremptory eyes
I instantly give up the goblet,
I tear it off my chest
and entrust it to that daunting beak.
Then, relieved,
I watch the eagle
fly to the centre of the river,
pause in the pulsing
of time and space
and dive down like stone,
down,
to immerse the goblet
and fill it with all the water it can hold.

In that instant I feel quartered
by immense forces,
I feel submerged and hidden,
then reassembled,
revealed,
contained by the form that comes back
into my hand.

Oh, it's just a glass of Styx,
a full-bodied black glittering
as turgid
as the juices of physical love.
Hypnotised,
I gaze and gaze
and for a moment I'm torn apart
by the mad impulse
to drink.

I clutch the goblet tight
to the point of pain,
now I'm suddenly frightened
my tears might drop in it
mixing me
with Hell,
but perhaps,
perhaps that's what needs to happen…

At this moment,
like in a crystal ball,
an unexpected vision takes shape.
I see it
I see it in the trembling dark water:
a curtain that opens,
the sculpture of memory
reanimated
and present.

I see myself as I am approaching Eros with the candle.
Oh impudent flame!
Oh unconscious game!
Did I really want to embrace
all life?
Did I?
Oh no, I have lied to myself!
I wasn't looking for consciousness
but for reassurance!
I didn't want to embrace life to the full
I only wanted a single piece of it:
JOY!
I only wanted Eros to be
a prince,
a man,

anything but the winged snake,
that's why I looked!

I broke the entirety
of Experience,
I filtered it in the agony
of Fear.

"Listen,"
I say to myself,
"the rumble of thunder
gets closer,
the breeze gets up
and becomes wind,
the empty rivers
flow again after the rain,
the dawn chorus
awakes after another night,
everything shakes itself to life,
everything transmutes.

Come my Soul,
let's not stand still
in joy,
let's not stand still
in pain,
let's move,
let's walk,
let's experience,
let's change."

VIII
Across the threshold

The latest task
is a pilgrimage to the
Underworld.
Aphrodite wants me to collect
Persephone's gift to Her.
I almost laughed when I was told:
do I get to die?
At last?

Some people struggle
to find the entrance
to the Underworld,
I simply hoisted myself
to the top of a tower,
vertiginous pinnacle,
immense quill of the soul.
I was already rocking myself
to nothingness,
I was already letting
gravity
suck me into its wide, open mouth,
when to my astonishment
the inanimate tower
broke into words.
Human, compassionate words
tumbled out of its weary stones
which became all wet
as from tears or dew.

Those words
touched my heart,
led me to the Underworld

through other, hidden paths,
while their counsel
kept echoing in my being
urging me
to unwaveringly focus on the task at hand.
Whatever happens I must not be diverted.

Oh, there is so much that won't be uttered
and in the inner silence
all the Underworld's rivers
seem to fluctuate
like in a wavering mirror
that clutches at the heart
and hides its beat.

I slowly slide over the threshold.
Beyond there's no frenzy:
for us mortals
the Underworld moves in slow motion,
we get drunk with the waiting,
we spy Being
in its excruciatingly slow transforming.

And each time I turn,
for an instant,
out of the corner of my
eye,
I believe I catch a glimpse
of Aphrodite leaning over the Styx.
She looks slow,
intent.
Large sweet eyes stolen by the waves,
garments gathered into a whisper,
braids tottering over the water,

one finger dipped in the tarry
reflection,
She writes something
I cannot see.

Vision or hallucination?

The evening is damp,
soft and cool,
there's only silence,
the distant, incessant swish
of souls,
the shuffling of Time.

IX
The Underworld

First Movement:
The Man

My hypnotic journey
through the Underworld
is confused
by the sour vision
of a man coming towards me.
He is lame
and so is his donkey
trailing behind.
Sticks and twigs
are falling like fossils
from the load on the animal's back.

Where is my strength?
Where does the violence I feel come from?

From the marrow of my bones
I resist the impulse
of picking up those bits of wood,
hanging hard on those bones
I won't help the man,
I won't be diverted!

Second Movement:
Charon

Charon,
burnt and ancient creature.

Who has dug your face
with barbed wire?
Will you take me across the river,
beyond,
in the portent of deities
who expect from me
what I cannot give?

I haven't come empty-handed:
I've got here the small
coin
with which your hairy
mouth
knows how to toy.
It's agony
but I will still throw it at you
and you will doggedly grab it mid-air
howling like the wolf you are.

I've paid the toll,
now your boat shapes down
in the water
by sinking as hard as
my weight.
I didn't know I was
so heavy,
so mortal.

Third Movement:
The Drowning

We slide forward
on the swollen tar of the Styx,
the dense scar
of the Universe.

I stare at my hands
as the only reference point left to me,
but when they tremble
I get swamped
by another vision:
there, in the fat tar
which is thirsty for fire,
I see a man
who screams,
who drowns.
I look at the man
and at my hands,
at my hands
and then at the man,
a strange, obtuse,
yet compelling
pity
ignites me.
I wish to save him
but I resist:
I spare my strength,
I spare my counsel,
I won't be diverted!

Fourth Movement:
The Fates

I disembark.
Beyond the Styx
one is in the heart of the
Underworld.
Oh yes, I feel like a dead woman.
I touch my body
as fragile as porcelain
yet still containing my soul…
I feel the uncertainty
of the time left to live.
Then my sleepy youth
gets shaken awake
by the Fates.

Oh, here are the old women at the Loom!
Oh, I see them so clearly!
The Underworld is their den.
They weave,
they knot,
they cut all our vows.
They stop me with mellifluous gestures
of trepidation.
They beg for my help.
NO NO NO!
With my hands on my ears,
with eyes wide shut,
with my tongue glued
to the palate,
with the heart
in full turmoil,
I flee them.

This is not the power I seek!
NO!
I won't be diverted!

Fifth Movement:
Cerberus

Cerberus,
hateful three-headed dog,
monster,
putrefied creature,
you bar my path
with mouths
like funnels of pus,
with teeth
eaten by worms,
with growling pumped up by bloody
rage.
But I will pass.
You can't harm me.
I will throw you
the cake
that is better than
any leash.
And then I will hurry
like a pilgrim who doesn't want to see
the obscene brawl
of the heads,
each avid for that booty.
I'll for ever leave behind
your brutal,
frustrated yelps.

You Animal in my head,
din of thoughts and identities,
is it in order to achieve
the Silence
of your absence
that I have been tossing about
for ever?
You, guardian of the
Underworld,
are you my Prohibition?
Is it by overcoming you
that I can twitch
the curtains
and get a glimpse
of the fields at Spring?

X
Compulsion

Oh Persephone,
I thought you would receive me
with silky accents
and unbounded breasts,
with sisterly, dancing ankles
and the gift of a common
destiny.
Instead I have arrived
into the heart of the Underworld
to find that all is
silence
and I can't see You.

I lie on the naked ground,
eat modest food,
recognise the guiding dream,
become a fountain of wisdom,
a divine tongue-twister.

After so much struggle
I quieten down.
They say it is this way,
through quiet,
that we, mortals,
learn to solve the Gods'
riddles.

Oh Persephone,
was the right hand I was offered yours?
Was it your finger on my lips?
A sorceress' trick

or the chisel
by which I have been worked over?

All there is left to do
is collect your gift for Aphrodite.
It is a small, sumptuous
casket.
My duty is done,
with it clutched tight in my hands
I can start back.

But what if I opened this casket?
What might it contain?
Surely a beauty ointment
from Goddess to Goddess.
Oh, I will take a little for myself,
nobody will notice,
nobody will mind.
The crack in the lid
like tickle to the mind,
the blade of curiosity
like tickle to the fingers,
the game of compensation
like carousel
to the heart.

Oh, a small compensation
for all my troubles,
there won't be another,
if I don't redress things myself
who will do it for me?
Oh, a beauty ointment
in order to be almost as beautiful
as a Goddess,
beautiful in the seduction

of all speaking tongues,
in the joy of returning
to the world of the living.

And then?
And then nothing.

"Come on, Psyche," I say.
"Psyche! Open the casket!"

XI
Shame

The casket springs open
like a malignant mouth.
Oh the stink,
the foul air!
I scream
and swear
and writhe
like a trapped animal!
my guts are churning
and curdling,
my lungs are burning,
my throat's on fire,
I am gasping,
I cannot breathe!

I AM DYING.

How will I find my word?
My future?
My memory?
My grace?
All gone.

There's no return for me.
No more return.
I have learnt nothing.
There's only
one
one last feeling:
SHAME.

XII
Eros' Song

Oh Psyche,
Why look on the outside for beauty?
Why look for what you already possess?

Rise and meet me, my love,
awaken,
inherit yourself,
I have come to claim you!
The tree has grown to
full height,
the seed has yielded its blossoming,
singing heart,
the hands of the Gods
have robed you...

And now you will have to bear
Light.
Can you sustain the tumble
of Light
as much as the spear
of Darkness?

Can you sustain the pearly bell of my smile?

Pain
can enter even the heart of a God,
you have changed me:
through you I know Myself
and I am known.
The ripening of one being ripens a thousand others,

it is like the showing of countless
constellations
in the blinking, immense
sky.

Come, my love.
You are my homesickness,
my perfection and my flaws,
the divinity and the humanity.
Oh, come to our
eternal dance,
come to our
wedding.
The things that were
have passed
and a new cycle,
a new beginning
is for ever knocking at the door.

ACKNOWLEDGEMENTS

I am very grateful to many people who have given me support and advice during the writing of this book.

In particular I wish to thank my partner and fellow poet Peter Huitson for his untiring involvement, enthusiasm and loving support. If I have learnt something of the difficult art of editing I owe it chiefly to him.

I also would like to thank Dan Holloway from Silverwood Books for his most valuable comments and I am grateful to John Bond and all the people at Whitefox Publishing Services for their wonderful, professional work in the production and launching of the book.

Finally my thanks go to a handful of people who have sustained me steadily through their understanding and love of my poetry: first and foremost Frank Seethaler, then Maggie Kafton, Donna Stewart, Nigel Hamilton, Angela Blesky, Jonathan Harris, Adriana Sabbadin, Roger Tickner, Alexandra Buist and Brigitte Spreeuwenberg.